9

CRITICAL TRUTHS YOU MUST KNOW ABOUT THE ENDTIMES

Don Kremer

D1319599

Nine Critical Truths You Must Know

Numeric references are scripted in digital characters contrary to traditional grammatical style for the sake of visual clarity.

ISBN 979-8-8325468-2-7

Don Kremer
vcfpdk@aol.com

DEDICATED TO HANS KOENIG
WHO WAS SUDDENLY TAKEN
WHILE I WAS WRITING THIS BOOK.

To Hans: "A relentless warrior of light."
A co-laborer in the
Gospel with me for 20 years
into Ghana, Africa.

March 3, 1952 to May 9, 2022

THE TABLE OF CONTENTS

INTRODUCTION

NINE CRITICAL TRUTHS ABOUT THE ENDTIMES YOU MUST KNOW

In 70 A.D. the Roman army invaded Jerusalem and slaughtered every Jew they could find: men, women, and children. Those who survived, fled to the mountains. From that time forward, their generations remained scattered throughout the nations.

In 1941, the demon-possessed Nazi army was slaughtering the Eastern European Jews by the multiples of thousands. The Jews, as a matter of survival, escaped into the forest with whatever they could carry by hand. This remarkable story is documented in a movie called "Defiance" and tells the account of the Bielski brothers who helped 1,200 Jews survive in the wilderness for years to escape Hitler's scourge.

In fact, this generation stands on the precipice of the last two prophetic events ready to be fulfilled before the Book of Revelation opens. As such, these are the end of days, not of mankind, but when God finally and ultimately judges the entity of evil and those who practice unrighteousness.

Even more incredible is the fact that you are chosen by the providence of God for such a time as this to turn many from their paths leading to eternal damnation.

What you are about to encounter is Nine Critical Truths you must know in these last days. With all certainty, 70 A.D. and 1941 will be repeated. Knowing theses critical truths is the difference between life and death. Like a bomb technician staring at a circuitry of wires, there is no margin for error. In the same way, the following truths contain no ambiguity. They are definitive and absolute.

What Exactly Are These Nine Truths?

In **Critical Truth #1**, you will learn about the Five Cycles of Evil found in Scripture. Currently, we are nearing the end of the 4th Cycle—the most hideous and loathsome of all five. It is this cycle where ¼ of mankind is killed in what is known as "The Tribulation". It is also the time for the return of Jesus Christ who rescues His people in an event called the "Rapture".

8

In **Critical Truth #2**, you will learn the precise access to the only prescription Jesus gave for power against the violent manifestations of Satan's demonic authority. This is critically important if you are going to survive the coming days.

In **Critical Truth #3**, you will learn about the specific prophecies that apply only to this generation. There are three of them; all three have been fulfilled. We are NOW facing the final two steps before the Book of Revelation opens.

In **Critical Truth #4**, the Seven Seals of Revelation are carefully explained. They have specific timeframes that you must know in order for you to plan for you and your loved ones. Miss this, and you'll miss your only opportunity for survival.

In **Critical Truth #5**, you will learn the four prophetic markers that prove the definitive identity of Antichrist. The prophetic insights surrounding this person will leave no question in your mind as to who he is—the most diabolic person who has ever existed that stands in a class of evil all his own. Without any uncertainty, his identity is clearly revealed by Bible prophecy. You likely know him by his name.

In **Critical Truth #6**, you will discover God's criteria for the selection of the Saints at the precise moment of His coming. In contrast to the generations before us who lived out their full years of life, this generation is an "interrupted" generation. It is intersected by the coming of the Lord as an emergency rescue or no one on earth would survive. For this reason, Jesus sets forth a clear warning in His parable of the Ten Virgins that apply "only" to our generation. Surprisingly, not all who claim to be a Christian will be taken in the rapture.

In **Critical Truth #7**, you will learn the specific factors needed to identify the next two events looming on the horizon right now. Currently, the Middle East is a boiling caldron of prophecy that soon opens the Book of Revelation. Keep your eyes on Israel. She is the key that sets things into motion.

In **Critical Truth #8**, you will understand what you should be doing right NOW in order to prepare according to God's timetable. What you do NOW determines if you will be a martyr of Antichrist, or a survivor until Jesus comes.

In **Critical Truth #9,** pertaining to those left behind, you will learn what happens to them *after* the Rapture. Some will give their lives to Jesus. But for those who receive the Mark of the Beast, it is utter chaos with the irreversible consequences of eternal damnation. Those who take the Mark of the Beast and worship his image have only 1,335 days more to live— if they survive the judgments of God.

How Could So Many Be Wrong for So Long?

In 52 AD, the Christians of Thessalonica sent word to the Apostle Paul because they were concerned that they had missed the Rapture of the church. They based their conclusion upon the heavy Roman persecution of all Christians. As a result, Paul wrote them two letters (I and II Thessalonians) and explained the sequence regarding the Endtimes. He reminded them of his teachings when he was with them in person that detailed the order.

Aside from Jesus, among all the teachers and prophets of the Bible, Paul is the only person whose writings "summarize" the Endtimes concerning the sequence of its order.

Although the Apostle John wrote the Book of Revelation, he never "explained" its events—he simply wrote what he heard and saw. Even Daniel did not understand what Gabriel, the angel, revealed to him concerning the events reaching into the very day in which we live (Daniel 12:8-9).

I Peter 4:7 was written in 63 AD. In his letter, Peter said, "The end of all things is near…"

Even though Peter and Paul felt the coming of the Lord was soon, more than 1,965 years have passed and still Jesus has not returned.

If Paul knew what signs to look for, how could he, being a premiere apostle who learned His Gospel and insights directly from Jesus, miss the timing of this critically important event by nearly two millenniums? The answer is simple: Certain keys were not revealed by God until the time was due.

11

The Book of Revelation, for instance, was written in 96 A.D., nearly 44 years *after* Paul wrote his letters to the Thessalonians—a full 28 years *after* he was martyred. Only in the Book of Revelation (and in no other prophecies) were specific events disclosed. (These will be covered in the following chapters.) Additionally, by the time John wrote the Book of Revelation, all the original Apostles had been martyred.[1]

In Revelation, a critically important fact was divulged for the first time that reaches into "our generation", namely that there was yet to come *another* Beast Empire—the 7th Empire—for a total of eight Beast Empires in all.

Only the Book of Revelation speaks of the 7th Beast Empire, an empire of great mystery—that is, until it came into existence in 1933. But it would take 1,837 years to be revealed *after* it was first announced in Revelation.

Prior to the Book of Revelation, the writings of Daniel, Isaiah, Zechariah, Jeremiah, and Ezekiel, were generally considered the most read prophecies about the Endtimes. Even so, none of them mention the 7th Beast Empire or its identity.

Daniel's Prophecies

Daniel's prophecies chiefly focused upon the periods of Israel's captivity by various heathen nations described as *Beast Empires*.

---

[1] John was the only apostle who was not martyred. He lived until the age of 100 before dying of natural causes.

At the time he wrote his prophecies, the first two Beast Empires were historic: Egypt and Assyria. Accordingly, Daniel's prophecies encompass the time *starting* from *his day* and reach forward to the Beast Empires of *our generation*—specifically the 8th.[2] However, Daniel's writings do not reveal *all* the events exclusive to us right now. Therefore, in order to gain a comprehensive understanding of the Endtimes, multiple prophecies from various books in both the Old Testament and New Testament must be considered.

Written For Us Today

Here we are today and still Jesus has not yet returned. What evidence exists that makes us any different than the generations before us who claimed the urgency of Jesus' return?

You are about to make that discovery.

Something is happening as never before: the universal Body of Christ in every nation among all people across all denominations are saying the same thing: "Jesus is coming soon."

Subtle as that may be, it is a major sign (but not the only one). For when the Saints across all nations speak as one voice in agreement, we must turn our attention to this unified voice and listen. Jesus said His sheep would hear His voice (John

---

[2] Daniel's prophecies begin with Israel's captivity under Babylon but do not include the first two Beast Empires, Egypt and Assyria. Our generation has experienced one Beast Empire, the 7th, and soon, the 8th. There are eight Beast Empires in all: Egypt, Assyria, Babylon, Medo-Persia, Greece, Rome, Nazi Germany, and the 8th—a confederation of ten nations under Antichrist.

10:27). Therefore, when the universal voice of Christ's people say the same thing, it is proof that His voice, through the Holy Spirit, is speaking for His people to get ready.

The reality is this: you are in the exit generation—THE chosen generation. Know for certain that you will see Antichrist take his seat in the newly built temple in Jerusalem and declare himself to be God Almighty.

Even more exciting is the fact that you are the generation that will see the return of Jesus Christ! You are, therefore, chosen of God. The fact that you are living at this time of humanity proves you are selected by God to bring unheralded glory to His name. You do not randomly exist by mere probability!

> **Your eyes have seen my unformed substance; and in Your book were all written the days that were ordained for me, when as yet there was not one of them.** Psalm 139:16

At this very moment, our generation is poised at the starting line before the final two prophecies blast into motion that opens the Book of Revelation. Soon and very soon, the domino effect begins. If you understand these prophecies, you will be able to recognize and correlate specific world events leading to their fulfillment.

In the following pages, you will learn about the Nine Critical Truths to equip you for specific events that are forming right now. These prophetic events have no salute toward denominational preference. It is the plain, simple, and unadulterated raw Word of God without bias or obscure interpretation.

God is Faithful to Truth

Keep this important truth about God in the forefront of your thinking: He is unwaveringly true to Himself. He is the Way, the Truth, and the Life. He is not a champion of anyone's pet doctrines that deviate from the integrity of His Word. We may be His Saints, but our obligation, regardless of any denominational preference, is to meet HIS standard of truth—not our concept of truth based upon personal philosophy, logic, tradition, or denominational persuasion.

Today, we are at the juncture in time where error is deadly. Therefore, we must be prudent enough to test everything we believe by the standard of His truth—the Bible. We cannot afford fallacious doctrines that lead us into disaster.

The importance of your witness in this generation is alarming. Statistically speaking, only one of every four people you pass on the street are saved. Conversely, this means three of them are eternally damned unless they receive Jesus Christ. Some of them could even be your family members. And even among those who are saved, very few are actually serving the Lord with their whole heart.

15

Three Precautions

In whatever Christian perspective you stand, give consideration to these **"three overlapping precautions"**. As previously stated, doctrinal error will cost you your life and for some, their eternity. It takes courage to let "truth" have its way. It can get uncomfortable, and it is challenging.

First, be courageous enough to test everything you believe by God's Word. Do not assume that the doctrines you have espoused all your life are true until **you** prove them to yourself through God's Word, the Bible. You might be surprised at what you discover.

Second, as you might have realized, many people tend to formulate their beliefs based upon the criteria of their logic. But remember: not all truth is logical and not all logic is truthful. Therefore, recheck everything you believe by God's Word—even the simplest of your assumptions. It is crucial at this hour that you know "why" you believe what you believe by using the proof of Scripture as the sole instrument of verification. Knowing that the Bible never contradicts truth, test the construction of your doctrinal reasoning that is joined to your personal philosophy to see if it agrees with God's truth.

Third, avoid the assumption that something is true based upon popular consensus or its repetitive recitals until you prove it by God's Word.

> Now the Berean Jews were of more noble character than those in Thessalonica, for they received the message with great eagerness and examined the Scriptures every

day to see if what Paul said was true. Acts
17:17 NIV

Examples of Common Presumptions

Let me give a few examples of what I am talking about by posing some questions: How many angels fell with Lucifer (Satan) when he was cast out of Heaven? The common answer: one third. The truth: nowhere in the Bible does it give a number or percentage of the angels that fell with him. This is an example where repetitive phrases that are spoken enough times become accepted as truth when in fact it is error. This is why you must "prove" what you believe.

The presumption that one-third of the angels fell with Satan comes from the wrongly applied verse out of Revelation 12:4:

His tail drew a third of the stars of heaven and threw them to the earth. And the dragon stood before the woman who was ready to give birth, to devour her Child as soon as it was born. Revelation 12:4

The context of the above Scripture has nothing to do with Satan's fall. It is an event when Satan, enraged with his obsession to destroy Israel, comes to the earth between the 3rd and 4th Seals of Revelation. He, along with his dark minions, begin a frenzied search to hunt down the 144,000 Jews—the First Fruits of Israel.

Here is another common presumption: Demons and fallen angels are one and the same. A fact of Scripture regarding the characteristics of angels, both holy and unholy, show they have the ability to change from a 4th dimension spiritual form to a 3rd dimension physical form. By comparison, demons cannot change their forms.

In the Genesis 6 account, for instance, fallen angels left their spiritual domain, took on flesh, and went into the daughters of men. Satan's intent was to create a hybrid race of people in order to intercept the pedigree lineage of humanity through which the Messiah, Jesus Christ, would come. In the book of Jude, we are told that God chained these extraordinary untamable angels in the regions of the dark to prevent them from doing it again.

> And angels who did not keep their own domain but abandoned their proper dwelling place, these He has kept in eternal restrain under darkness for the judgment of the great day, 7 just as Sodom and Gomorrah and the cities around them, since they in the same way as these angels indulged in sexual perversion and went after strange flesh, are exhibited as an example in undergoing punishment of eternal fire. Jude 1:6-7

Because demons cannot change their state of existence, a demon needs a physical body to express itself, and will even live in a pig if it has no other options (Mark 5:1-20). The origin of demons is not given in Scriptures.

Again, this is an example of presumption. And when it comes to the subject of the Endtimes, presumptions, assumptions, logic, and false conclusions constitute a plague of misinformation.

Common Presumptions About the Endtimes

"The Seven Year Tribulation Period" is perhaps one of the most erroneous phrases about the Endtimes. There is a seven-year-period folded into the 2,595 days of Revelation, and there is a Tribulation. But there is no 7-Year Tribulation Period.

Based upon Scripture, the time duration of the "Tribulation Period" is not revealed to mankind. What we know by Scripture is this: the Tribulation is less than seven years in length and it does not begin until the 4th Seal of Revelation. It ends abruptly upon the return of Jesus Christ at the time of the 6th Seal. Further, we can know the exact the day when the 4th Seal opens based upon the exact day the 1st Seal opens. And we can know the exact day the 1st Seal opens based upon the moment Israel signs a 7-Year Peace Pact. But…we do not know when the 5th Seal opens because that is an event exclusively occurring in Heaven and is not seen on the earth.

If the time of the 6th Seal was revealed by Scripture, we would know the exact day of Jesus' return because He comes at the end of the 6th Seal.

While all that might sound like a random cluster of abstract information, don't worry. Before you finish this book, everything will be simplistic and easy to understand.

Pre-Trib, Mid-Trib, or Post-Trib?

Another ubiquitous error among a majority of Christians, belongs to those who configure the time of Jesus' return (the Rapture) in relationship to the Tribulation Period.

Scripture NEVER correlates the timing of the Rapture in connection to the Tribulation. This teaching did not emerge until about 1830 by a man named John Nelson Darby in his invention of biblical interpretation called "Dispensational Theology". Consequently, for the first 1,800 years of the Christian church, the timing of the Rapture was placed in relevant position to God's wrath. Why? Because God will not punish the Righteous along with the Wicked. Therefore, before the fury of God's wrath is poured out, He first removes the Saints by an event called the Rapture.

The Tribulation Period and God's Wrath

This is yet another serious mistake that has produced a great deal of confusion. Many Christians blend God's wrath and the Tribulation into one coinciding event. In fact, they are two distinct occasions within Revelation.

The Tribulation of the Saints is exclusively the work of Antichrist against all who refuse to take the Mark of the Beast and worship his image.

In contrast, God's wrath is His judgments against the wicked masses on the earth and the despotic hosts of demonic swarms including Satan "after" God removes the Saints by means of the Rapture.

The precise time of the Tribulation begins at the 4th Seal when the False Prophet orders everyone to receive the Mark of the Beast and worship Antichrist. From that point forward until Jesus comes, ¼ of mankind is killed for refusing to worship Antichrist. This defines the Tribulation period.

The Wrath of God, different than the Tribulation, does not begin until the 1st Trumpet Judgment which is after the close of the 7th Seal. From that moment forward, the fury of God's wrath is poured out until the close of the 7th Bowl Judgment in a duration of time that is slightly less than 1,290 days.

When you get into Chapter 4, all of this is carefully explained in simplistic terms; it is rather straightforward and uncomplicated.

Moving Forward

As you read each of the Nine Critical Truths, keep this in mind: there are not multiple truths about the Endtimes. Scripture speaks one truth, not variations of truth. The Bible never offers multiple choice options about truth. If there are varying opinions, it proves there are varying errors

And Now, You

Because you are here at this time, you are part of the Exit Generation. To you it is granted the understanding and insight of things about to happen that previous generations did not know because the Lord did not reveal it to them since it did not apply to them as it does to us in this generation.

In Daniel's day, for instance, the end was NOT near, and the disclosures about the Endtimes were *sealed* and NOT understood. It is just the opposite today. Today, the end IS near, and the understanding and insights are given by the Holy Spirit who speaks only ONE truth:

> But as for me [Daniel], I heard [the prophecy the angel was giving] but did not understand; so I said, "My lord, what will be the outcome of these events?" 9 <u>And he said, "Go your way Daniel for these words will be kept secret and sealed until the end time."</u> Daniel 12:8-9 (Square brackets and underline inserted by the author for clarity of context.)

> And he [an angel sent from Jesus] said to me [the apostle John], "<u>Do not seal up the words of the prophecy</u> of this book, for the time is near." Revelation 22:10 (Square brackets and underline inserted by the author for clarity of context.)

Nine Critical Truths You Must Know

The truths you are about to discover are vitally important at this hour. They are basic, but they are challenging. It takes courage to let truth reprove error and expose the many presumptions about the Endtimes that are commonly embraced by this generation.

May the Spirit of God's truth, the Holy Spirit, give you understanding in order to see the depths of all He has planned. Let us not be taken by surprise, for He has given us clear insights all the way to the end.

> Wisdom is supreme—so get wisdom. And whatever else you get, get understanding.
> (Proverbs 4:7 HCSB)

CHAPTER 1
CRITICAL TRUTH #1

Five Cycles of Evil

In this Critical Truth, the timeline of humanity points decisively to this generation. In that regard, your existence is not a random occurrence. By the divine purpose and intention of God's wisdom, you are chosen to be here at the greatest moment of all time since Adam's fall. The question that emerges for each of us is this: what is our purpose relative to the day in which we live? To answer that question, it is needful to understand what God says about the immediate future that each of us are about to experience.

Two personalities preponderate in our generation: God and Satan. Sounds simple and trite, but this is the time they war over the world and all who live in it. This is the time that God deals with Satan and his reign of evil, once and for all. For that reason, we are approaching an epoch such as the world has never seen before in all of humanity.

Chronicled throughout Scripture is the scattered evidence of five distinct cycles of evil[3], or conversely, five major efforts of Satan to establish his dominion on the earth. For that reason, we should know something about this archon of evil.

Satan Before His Fall

In the Book of Ezekiel, we are given a detailed description of Satan, one of God's most magnificent angels—Lucifer , meaning "Light Bearer":

> You were in Eden, the garden of God; every precious stone was your covering: the ruby, the topaz and the diamond; the beryl, the onyx and the jasper; the lapis lazuli, the turquoise and the emerald; and the gold, the workmanship of your settings and sockets, was in you. On the day that you were created they were prepared. 14 You were the anointed cherub who covers, and I placed you {there.} You were on the holy mountain of God; you walked in the midst of the stones of fire. 15 You were blameless in your ways from the day you were created until unrighteousness was found in you. Ezekiel 28:13-15

---

[3] See appendix 1 for a detailed explanation of each of the Five Cycles of Evil

The glory of this arch angel can only be imagined relative to his position stationed at the throne of God. He was the anointed cherub (winged angel) that led the myriads upon myriads of angels in the worship of God—the highest most holy activity in Heaven.

How long he occupied this position is not given in Scripture. But at some point he began thinking more highly of himself than he should have. In pride, he exalted himself above God and lusted for the admiration and glory that belongs exclusively to God. This was a criminal offense of the utmost sin that resulted in him being expelled from Heaven.

> I am the LORD, that is My name; I will not give My glory to another, nor My praise to graven images. Isaiah 42:8

1st Cycle of Evil

In the 1st Cycle of Evil when Satan is cast to earth, Isaiah records the depth of Satan's pride that toppled this glorious arch angel:

> How you have fallen from heaven, O star of the morning, son of the dawn! You have been cut down to the earth, you who have weakened the nations! 13 But you said in your heart, "I will ascend to heaven; I will raise my throne above the stars of God, and

I will sit on the mount of assembly in the recesses of the north. 14 I will ascend above the heights of the clouds; I will make myself like the Most High." Isaiah 14:12-14

Jesus said of Satan:

"I was watching Satan fall from heaven like lightning." Luke 10:18b

Ever since Satan's fall in the 1st Cycle of Evil, he has maintained a relentless pursuit to rule the universe and be worshipped as God.

After he was cast to the earth, he encountered one of God's most precious creation that was made in the image of God—man.

It was Adam, the first man, to whom God gave dominion and authority over all the earth. Satan wanted Adam's position in order to transform the earth so that he would be worshipped.

Then God said, "Let Us make man in Our image, according to Our likeness; and let them rule over the fish of the sea and over the birds of the sky and over the cattle and

27

over all the earth, and over every creeping thing that creeps on the earth." Genesis 1:26

2nd Cycle of Evil

The story of Satan's approach to Eve in the Garden of Eden is well documented in Scripture where ultimately, both Adam and Eve fell into sin (Genesis 3:1-7). At that moment, creation, including mankind, took on the nature of Satan's fallen condition. Consequently, when Adam surrendered his authority by sin, in the 2nd Cycle of Evil, Satan commenced his global conquest to be worshipped as God.

3rd Cycle of Evil

The global flood of Noah's day occurred because God spoiled the 3rd Cycle of Evil. This was when Satan almost completely polluted the human race through human hybridization with fallen angels in order to destroy the line of pedigree humanity through which Jesus would come. (Genesis 3:15; Genesis 6:1-6).

4th Cycle of Evil and Its Current State of Evil

The 4th Cycle of Evil starts from the Tower of Babel and reaches into our day, and ends with the 7th Bowl Judgment of Revelation.

Going back to the Tower of Babel, within 300 years after Noah's sons stepped from the Ark, mankind grew pridefully self-sufficient and no longer acknowledged God as their very source of life. At that time, the entire populace of mankind was one language with unimpeded communication. The power of their agreement made it possible for them to accomplish almost anything they could imagine. But, they were moving in a direction away from God toward self-destruction. Consequently, God confounded the languages of the people and scattered them throughout the world.

As previously stated, the duration of the 4th Cycle of Evil commences from the time of their scattering and reaches into the very day we live. Accordingly, the Endtime events that Jesus detailed in the chapters of Matthew 24 and 25 are events occurring during the 4th Cycle of Evil. It is a period of time that encompasses the Rapture of the church all the way to the first day of Jesus' millennial reign. Accordingly, the 4th Cycle also encompasses the entire period of the Book of Revelation. This includes the time Antichrist goes into the temple in Jerusalem and declares himself to be God. The 4th Cycle of Evil then celebrates a climactic moment when it seems that Satan momentarily accomplishes his goal to be worshipped as God, but only by those who have no love for the truth.

Satan's victory, however, along with his cohort, Antichrist, is short lived. Antichrist's reign lasts only 1,290 days from the time he enters the newly built temple in Jerusalem until Jesus destroys him at the time of the Battle of Armageddon. Antichrist, along with the False Prophet, are then cast into the Lake of Fire to commence their eternal punishment. Following that, every soldier of Antichrist's army is cast into

Hell.[4] Approximately 46 days later, (according to biblical prophecy) Satan is locked in the Abyss[5] for 1,000 years. This ends the 4th Cycle of Evil and begins the 1,000-Year Rule of Jesus Christ on earth.

5th Cycle of Evil

At the end of the Millennial reign of Jesus, the 5th Cycle of Evil commences when Satan is released from the Abyss to gather the untested unproven peoples of the earth who were born throughout the time of the Millennium.

This final great battle ends when Satan and his followers are cast directly into the Lake of Fire. In this final conflict, Satan and his constituents are destroyed by fire from Heaven (Revelation 20:9).

Today, you stand on the precipice of the 7-Year Period of Revelation—the final sequence of the 4th Cycle of Evil—the most cataclysmic time of all.

It is the events within the 4th Cycle of Evil that Paul addresses in his letters to the Thessalonians where his instructions set the concise order by which things will occur.

> "Let no one in any way deceive you, for it [the coming of the Lord starting with the Rapture] will not come unless the apostasy

---

[4] The Lake of Fire is the final abode of all evil. At the end of the Millennial Reign of Jesus, (after the final battle of the 5th Cycle), Jesus holds court at the White Throne Judgment. This is where the books are opened and the wicked spirits and the souls in Hell are brought before the throne of the Lord. The degree of their punishment is weighed against the works of their evil.

[5] The Abyss and the Bottomless Pit are different names for the same place.

[a great falling away from the truth] comes first, and the man of lawlessness is re-vealed, the son of destruction..." II Thessalonians 2:3 (Square brackets inserted by the author for clarity of context.)

The Prophesied Apostacy Is Here

Currently there is apostacy in many churches along with a general saturated wickedness in society. Crime, for instance has grown exponential in major cities like Chicago which is the murder capital of the world.

Moreover, various churches and denominations have radically departed from God's fundamental positions of righteousness and now embrace a new definition for love that merely winks at sin" and even endorses fundamentally immoral practices within the congregations of its people.

Today, more than ever before, a fast-growing number of liberal churches deny God's Word, the Bible, as an absolute unchanging truth for all generations. They see it as something written in the cultural era of the Apostles and Prophets instead of being inspired by the Holy Spirit. Accordingly, in the modern perspective, God's truths and principles are debatable. Further, they are viewed through the lens of social interpretation, situational ethics, and then subsequently refitted to this generation's ideology.

Falling deeper into darkness, society shamelessly embraces all forms of moral decadence which is now protected by law. Liberal denominations openly sanction such lifestyles including the ordination of clergy that promote and celebrate them.

Sadly, many people suffer great conflict when it comes to their sexual identity. It is here that the heart of Jesus breaks for those caught in such turbulence. As such, to minimize the disparity between one's physical anatomy and their self-perceived gender, the physical appearance is altered by a series of medical procedures that *superficially* changes their appearance from one gender to another. It is benignly called, "gender reassignment surgery" known as GRS.

Despite such deep-seated conflicts where one's new physical identity clashes with their mental identity, the rate of suicide is exponentially high according to a well-documented report published by the UCLA Williams Institute School of Law (August 2020):

"Research has shown a high prevalence of suicidal behavior among LGB people.

"A 2016 review of research found that 17% of LGB [Lesbian, Gay, and Bi-sexual] adults had attempted suicide during their lifetime, compared with 2.4% of the general U.S. population. A recent report from the Generations Study, a nationally representative study of cisgender [denoting or relating to a person whose sense of personal identity and gender corresponds with their birth sex] LGB people, found that LGBQ people who experienced conversion therapy were at higher risk for suicide behavior compared with their peers who didn't undergo the practice.

"LGBQ people were 92% more likely to think about suicide, 75% more likely to plan suicide, and 88% more likely to actually attempt suicide that resulted in no or minor injury.

"The 2015 U.S. Transgender Survey (USTS), conducted by the National Center for Transgender Equality, found that the prevalence of suicide thoughts and attempts among transgender adults is significantly higher than that of the U.S. general population. 82% of respondents reported ever seriously thinking about suicide in their lifetimes, while 48% had done so in the past year. 40% reported attempting suicide at some point in their lifetimes, and 7% had attempted it in the past year.

"A 2014 report found that LGBTQ youth are at heightened risk for suicidal outcomes, but risk varies based on sex and race/ethnicity. In general, LGBTQ youth were three times more likely than non-LGBQ youth to contemplate suicide, make a suicide plan, harm themselves, or attempt suicide compared to non-LGBTQ youth. LGBTQ females had higher prevalence of suicide thoughts, attempts, and self-harm than their male counterparts."[6]

In order for today's society and the Emergent Church to reach a continuity of agreement, certain truths defining God's unchanging character must be avoided or reinterpreted. Accordingly, the dark philosophy of the "Woke Generation"

---

[6] Quoted in part: https://williamsinstitute.law.ucla.edu/press/suicide-prevention-media-alert/

fundamentally denies the absolution of truth—an *obstacle* in the system of their evolving moral code.

> But speaking the [God's] truth in love, we are to grow up in all aspects into Him who is the head, even Christ. Eph 4:15 (Square brackets inserted by the author for clarity.)

In the Emergent[7] Church's view of "love", love is defined according to what anyone wants it to be. Consequently, the factors of truth that define love are eliminated in order to fit the situational ethics so as to remove or lessen the moral conviction of sin.

> But realize this, that in the last days difficult times will come. 2 For men will be lovers of self, lovers of money, boastful, arrogant, revilers, disobedient to parents, ungrateful, unholy, 3 unloving, irreconcilable, malicious

---

[7] The Emergent Church is systematized in its approach to accommodate a modern generation whose developing new social mores are radical departures from core central values of Christian apostolic doctrines. They do this by first minimizing or rejecting the inerrant Word of God and then redefining the Scriptures to be the new standards of the day rather than teaching the generation to meet the standards of Scripture. Such churches have soul-driven appeal, are usually modern-techno in their approach, and place little demand on Scriptural conformity. Thus, they fulfill the prophetic claims of Paul who said, *"For the time will come when they will not endure sound doctrine; but wanting to have their ears tickled, they will accumulate for themselves teachers in accordance to their own desires..."* 2 Timothy 4:3

gossips, without self-control, brutal, haters of good, 4 treacherous, reckless, conceited, lovers of pleasure rather than lovers of God, 5 holding to a form of godliness, although they have denied its power; avoid such men as these. II Timothy 3:1-5

Even though they have a "form" of godliness, their doctrines are largely emotional-based and sense-feeling oriented. The Gospel message is configured to appeal to their audience so that the truth does not offend. In such churches, God's presence is synthesized, not actual. The stage effects used to create the faux atmosphere of smoke and lights as an ambiance of His holy presence is nothing more than something that is "feeling-oriented".

While such fabrications have an appealing religious sense of awe and mystique, it is couched in the unregenerated soul of man, not the Spirit of God. In such churches, the Lord has removed the candlestick of His light and glory. Sadly, most people who attend such gatherings have no idea that His presence is repressed or altogether absent.

They will maintain the outward appearance of religion but will have repudiated its power. So avoid people like these. II Timothy 3:5 (The Net Bible)

Righteousness demands repentance, and repentance is defined as conforming to the standard of God's truth. In most cases, such demands in the Emergent Church is viewed as bigotry. As a result, the Gospel message is blanched. Sin is pampered by using secular-compassion that is set in the philosophy of "change toward Christlikeness at your own pace"—whatever Christlikeness looks like to them.

Paul confronted these very issues in his letters to the Corinthians. They casually tolerated various types of sin, some of which were considered scandalous even by the secular world. As a result, their gatherings were polluted which in turn grieved the Holy Spirit.

Wickedness in the World

In our culture today, laws exist to license those things that God deems as abominations, such as abortion, the LBTQ agenda, non-gender identity, and gender reassignment—all of which are celebrated as the new enlightenment of a progressive society.

Accordingly, Gender identity is now defined as what each person describes themselves to be. This perversion is now taught to the fragile and unguarded minds of children as early as the elementary grades.

Noah and Lot

The days of Noah depict total depravity and wickedness, while the days of Lot depict saturated sexual perversion now present in this generation.

Noah and Lot were separated by 500 years in time. But when the characterisms of both come together as they are in this generation, Jesus said it marks the season of His return.

> Woe to those who call evil good, and good evil; who substitute darkness for light and light for darkness; who substitute bitter for sweet and sweet for bitter! Isaiah 5:20

> And just as it happened in the days of Noah, so will it also be in the days of the Son of Man 27 *people* were eating, they were drinking, they were marrying *and* they were being given in marriage, until the day that Noah entered the ark, and the flood came and destroyed them all. 28 It was the same as happened in the days of Lot: they were eating, they were drinking, they were buying, they were selling, they were planting, *and* they were building; 29 but on the day that Lot went out from Sodom it rained fire and brimstone from heaven and destroyed them all. 30 It will be just the same on the day that the Son of Man is revealed. Luke 17:26-30

The challenge for the true church today is holding the line of God's absolute truths juxtaposed to the "compromised churches" and the laws that endorse and protect those things which God finds disgraceful and offensive to His righteousness.

CHAPTER 2
CRITICAL TRUTH #2

Power To Defeat The Enemy

In this Critical Truth, you will learn about the power God has provided for you as a disciple of Jesus Christ. It is Satan's most feared weapon: the Baptism of the Holy Spirit.

The Baptism of the Holy Spirit is the Lord's prescription to "weaponize" His people against the greatest foe of all. For this reason, Satan has created a volume of false doctrine surrounding the truths related to the Holy Spirit's gift. To be clear, the Baptism of the Holy Spirit is a distinct event separate from the Holy Spirit's residence within the believer at the moment of salvation.

The Prescription for Power

The only prescription Jesus gave for *power* to be a witness is by one means: the Baptism of the Holy Spirit.[8] Without the Holy Spirit's gifting, the Christian is significantly less effective against forces of wickedness—especially at this hour

---

[8] The Baptism of the Holy Spirit is NOT required of any person for salvation. Salvation is based upon one's acceptance of Jesus Christ as their savior. There are some who erroneously assert that unless one is baptized in the Holy Spirit as recorded in Acts 2:4, he cannot be saved. Scripture does not support that claim.

as the translucent curtain between the 3rd and 4th dimensions lowers with a brazen display of demonic activity.

As previously stated in Chapter 1, the *days of Noah and Lot* are fully upon this generation. Iniquity has reached unprecedented levels and continues to increase exponentially without shame or humiliation as society moves progressively forward in the darkness.

Those baptized in the Holy Spirit, however, possess significant advantage over the enemy. This is because those who have the Holy Spirit's gifting possess massively greater measures of divine authority, power, and sensitivity to the Holy Spirit and His nine gifts. Accordingly, a major contrast between the churches today is seen by those who have power to stand against evil as compared to those who are merely academic in their faith.

Notably, churches embracing the Baptism of the Holy Spirit readily acknowledge the spiritual realm with a greater sense of acuity. Their confession of faith is more than the format of "word only". Rather, it is in the power and demonstration of the Holy Spirit that rips away the veil of Satan's hidden works.

> But you will receive <u>power</u> when the Holy Spirit has come upon you; and you shall be My witnesses both in Jerusalem, and in all Judea and Samaria, and even to the remotest part of the earth. Acts 1:8

Satan is a liar—the greatest deceiver throughout all of creation, the complete antithesis of God. The devil has locked entire denominations of the Christian faith with fear and confusion by creating logic-based controversy on the subject of the Baptism of the Holy Spirit.

To do that, he has instituted various doctrines in the format of his greatest deception: "Dispensational Theology"—a logic-based reasoning that many times results in the misapplication of God's Word. As a result, many Christians have disqualified this power and assigned it as something limited to the early church. To Scripturally repudiate that error, a few points of consideration need to be understood before this Critical Truth is further explained.

When Did the New Testament Covenant Begin?

Even though the Holy Spirit worked in and through righteous men and women throughout the ages starting from Adam, He could not take *permanent residence* within them *until* the blood of Christ was shed. This is because only Christ's blood can legally cleanse a person from sin and make his or her body a fit habitation for the Holy Spirit.

Now on the last day, the great {day} of the feast, Jesus stood and cried out, saying, "If anyone is thirsty, let him come to Me and drink. 38 He who believes in Me, as the Scripture said, From his innermost being will flow rivers of living water." 39 But this He

spoke of the Spirit, whom those who believed in Him were to receive; <u>for the Spirit
was not yet given</u> **[as an indwelling permanent resident]** <u>because Jesus was not yet
glorified.</u> John 7:37-39 (Square brackets underline and inserted by the author for clarity of context.)

Since John 7:39 confirms that the Holy Spirit had not been
given "as a permanent indwelling presence" to any person
prior to Jesus shedding His blood, the question presents itself
as to when the Holy Spirit was sent in order for the New Covenant of Christ to begin.

Most people think the church started on the day of Pentecost which was 50 days "after" the crucifixion of Jesus.
Again, this is another area of common presumption.

Few realize the additional steps Jesus needed to complete
after His crucifixion in order to ratify the New Covenant. Of
utmost importance, Jesus needed to send the Holy Spirit as
promised.

"But I tell you the truth, it is to your advantage that I go away; for if I do not go
away, the Helper will not come to you; but if
I go, I will send Him to you." John 16:7

The sending of the Holy Spirit is a marked definitive
event recorded in the Gospel of John. On the day Jesus sent
Him, the Holy Spirit instantly and simultaneously indwelt

every Christian as His temple and continues to do so for as many who receive Jesus as their Savior. But…according to Scripture, the Holy Spirit *could not be sent* by Jesus until three specific tasks were completed:

First, the crucifixion of Jesus had to be completed where His blood was shed for the redemption of mankind. As previously stated, only His blood can remove the stain of sin. The shed blood of bulls and sheep merely covered sin like a jacket over a red catsup stain on a white shirt.

Second, after Jesus's crucifixion, He descended into the heart of the earth where the Righteous Saints waited in Paradise for the confirmation that their sins were removed by Jesus' sacrifice.

Third, after Jesus presented Himself in Paradise, He then had to ascend to His Father in Heaven where He would be *reglorified* with the glory He had before the world was created.

Only after the completion of all three requirements could the Holy Spirit be sent to *permanently* indwell each Christian (John 7:38-39).

For those reasons, mankind waited for the pivotal event of Jesus' *reglorification,* an event that occurred on the third day *after* He was crucified.

Jesus affirmed this step in a prayer He spoke to the Father:

Now, Father, glorify Me together with Yourself, with the glory which I had with You before the world was. John 17:5

The Reglorification Explained

When Jesus came to the earth as the Messiah through the virgin, Mary, He set aside all the glory and virtue that belongs only to God. He then put on the flesh of mankind and took on the same limitations as any man, yet, without sin. He was tempted with every temptation (God in His glory cannot be tempted: James 1:13). He hungered, grew weary, was humiliated, tried by the courts of mere man, tortured, bled, and died.

Have this attitude in yourselves which was also in Christ Jesus,6 who, although He existed in the form of God, did not regard equality with God a thing to be grasped, 7 but emptied Himself, taking the form of a bond-servant, *and* being made in the likeness of men. 8 Being found in appearance as a man, He humbled Himself by becoming obedient to the point of death, even death on a cross. 9 For this reason also, God highly exalted Him, and bestowed on Him the name which is above every name, 10 so that at the name of Jesus every knee will bow, of those who are in heaven and on earth and under the earth, 11 and that every tongue will confess that Jesus Christ is Lord, to the glory of God the Father. Philippians 2:5-11

Therefore, He had to be made like His brethren in all things, so that He might become a merciful and faithful high priest in things pertaining to God, to make propitiation for the sins of the people. Hebrews 2:17

After Jesus was crucified, His ministry on earth was finished. He then commenced the final steps toward His reglorification.

But I tell you the truth, it is to your advantage that I go away; for if I do not go away [to be reglorified], the Helper will not come to you; but if I go, I will send Him to you [after Jesus is reglorified]. John 16:7 (Square brackets and underline inserted by the author for clarity of context.)

Because of the importance of Jesus sending the Holy Spirit, God made sure the event was definitively recorded in John 20:22.

Recounting the precise moment when the New Covenant was inaugurated, we must consider particular events given in Scripture beginning from the time Jesus was crucified on Friday, at 9:00 AM and until His death at 3:00 PM (Matthew

27:45), followed by the subsequent steps leading to His reglorification.

Jewish law dictates that the deceased cannot remain overnight without burial. Sympathetic to such law, Pilate gave permission to Joseph of Arimathea to have Jesus' body removed from the cross on Friday *before* sunset which was around 6:30 PM. Jesus was then placed in a tomb, specifically the tomb belonging to Joseph of Arimathea.

Every Friday at sunset, the Jewish Sabbath begins and continues until sunset on Saturday. According to Jewish law, no work can be done during the Sabbath. Therefore, the first opportunity to embalm Jesus' body was Sunday, the first day of the week.

On Sunday morning before sunrise, the 3rd day after Jesus' crucifixion[9], Mary Magdalene went to the tomb to prepare His body. To her great surprise, Jesus met her "in His *resurrected* state"—not His *reglorified* state. Ecstatic with joy, she clung to Him in celebration.

Again, at the time of her encounter, Jesus had not yet ascended to the Father for His "reglorification". He had just returned from being with the Saints in Paradise. By consequence, this means Jesus had not yet sent the Holy Spirit *as a*

---

[9] The Jewish culture typically refers to any part of a single day as a day . Thus Friday was the first day Jesus was in the center of the earth, Hades, speaking to the saints who awaited their redemption. Then, Saturday was the 2nd day, and Sunday before sunrise was the 3rd day. He meets Mary before sunrise and then again with 10 Apostles (Thomas was not there) on Sunday in the evening having been reglorified according to John 15:5 and John 20.

45

permanent indwelling resident to any Believer. Jesus confirms this needful step of His reglorification where John records the incident:

> Jesus said to her, "Stop clinging to Me, <u>for I have not yet ascended to the Father</u>; but go to My brethren and say to them, I ascend to My Father and your Father, and My God and your God." John 20:10 (Underline by author.)

On the same day Jesus met Mary at the tomb, He immediately afterward ascended to His father and was reglorified. All the virtue of His former glory that He put off when He came in the weakness of human flesh, He put back on in His glorified state—the glory that exclusively belongs to God.[10]

At evening time *on the same day after He met Mary at the tomb*, He returned from the Father in His *reglorified* state and suddenly appeared to His ten disciples that were hiding behind locked doors for fear of the Jews that associated them with Jesus. At the time He appeared to them, Judas was dead and Thomas, for some reason, was not present.

---

[10] [Jesus] who, being in the form of God, did not consider it robbery to be equal with God, 7 but made Himself of no reputation, taking the form of a bondservant, and coming in the likeness of men. 8 And being found in appearance as a man, He humbled Himself and became obedient to the point of death, even the death of the cross. Phil 2:6-8 NKJV

Scripture is careful to record this event because on this momentous occasion, Jesus sent the Third Person of the Trinity. He demonstrated the act of sending Him by breathing on them.

> So when it was evening on that day, the first {day} of the week, and when the doors were shut where the disciples were, for fear of the Jews, Jesus came and stood in their midst and said to them, "Peace {be} with you." 20 And when He had said this, He showed them both His hands and His side. The disciples then rejoiced when they saw the Lord. 21 So Jesus said to them again, "Peace {be} with you; as the Father has sent Me, I also send you." 22 And when He had said this, <u>He breathed on them and said to them, "Receive the Holy Spirit"</u>. John 20:19-22 (Underline by author.)

Simultaneous with that event, the Holy Spirit, in His omnipresence, took permanent residence in all believers *in* the earth—specifically in Paradise, *on* the earth, and *in* Heaven—in particular Enoch and Elijah—all at the same time. This decisive act officially inaugurated the New Covenant and it was at that historic moment that the church began.

It is interesting that the Greek word for *spirit* is *pneuma* from which we get the English word, pneumatic, meaning breath or air. Jesus purposely used this symbolism when sending the Holy Spirit.

What Defines the Church?

The definition of the church, from the Lord's perspective, is not based upon an address or the placard name of a denomination. It is based on one criteria only: if anyone has the Holy Spirit in them, they belong to Jesus. Conversely, the church is comprised of all people in Christ from every nation and culture who have the Spirit of Christ in them.

But if anyone does not have the Spirit of Christ, he does not belong to Him. Romans 8:9

Three Gifts of the Godhead

Jesus is the first gift that was given by the Father. When Jesus sent the Holy Spirit, the *second gift* of the Godhead was given. The *third gift* would not be given until the day of Pentecost,—the Holy Spirit's Baptism. The third gift is for all Believers starting from Pentecost to the day of Jesus' return.

Accordingly, the Father gave His gift—Jesus Christ; the Son gave His gift—the Holy Spirit; and the Holy Spirit gives His gift—the Baptism of the Holy Spirit. In this manner, all three persons of the Godhead are invested in the birth, sanctification, and maturation of each Saint.

Contrasting Evidence

Here is a contrasting point for consideration: It is plainly evident that the disciples received the *permanent indwelling presence* of the Holy Spirit when Jesus breathed on them in John 20:22, but....they had not received the *third gift, the baptism of the Holy Spirit* at that time. As previously stated, the Holy Spirit's gift would not be given until 47 days later on Pentecost.

Keep in mind that when Jesus gave His final instructions to the disciples, they were told to wait in Jerusalem until they received power even though they <u>had already received the permanent indwelling presence of the Holy Spirit</u>:

Gathering them together, He commanded them not to leave Jerusalem, but to wait for what the Father had promised, "Which," {He said} "you heard of from Me; 5 for John baptized with water, <u>but you will be baptized with the Holy Spirit not many days from now</u> **[even though they had already received His permanent indwelling presence].** 6 So when they had come together, they were asking Him, saying, "Lord, is it at this time You are restoring the kingdom to Israel?" 7 He said to them, "It is not for you to know times or epochs which the Father has fixed

by His own authority[11]; 8 <u>but you will receive power when the Holy Spirit has come upon you; and you shall be My witnesses both in Jerusalem, and in all Judea and Samaria, and even to the remotest part of the earth."</u>
Acts 1:4-8 (Square brackets and underline inserted by the author for clarity of context.)

Note The Differences

If **power** to be a witness comes to every Believer at the initial point of salvation when the Holy Spirit assumes permanent indwelling residence, then why did Jesus tell His disciples not to leave until they had received power? The answer is obvious: The power they needed can only come through the *Baptism of the Holy Spirit, or conversely speaking, by receiving the Holy Spirit's gift.* The proof of His baptism would be evidenced by the ability to speak in other tongues.

Space and context does not allow all the Scriptural proofs concerning this to be detailed in this book, but suffice it to say that when the disciples received the Baptism of the Holy Spirit, they were given "power" to do the works of God, which, in turn, would be a continual proving witness (evidence) of Jesus.

This is clearly shown by the contrast in their boldness to share Christ. Following that, they walked in signs, wonders,

---

[11] This event would be fulfilled at the 6th Trumpet Judgment of Revelation and celebrated at the time of the 7th Trumpet Judgment.

and miracles which God performed through them "after" the ascension of Jesus.

Prior to the event of them receiving power, (which initially occurred on the day of Pentecost), it must be assumed that they *did not possess* the "power" Jesus told them they were to wait for. Why is this important?

The words *witness* and *martyr* are the same word in Greek—the language of the New Testament[12].

Consider the original apostles' lack of power in the Garden of Gethsemane when they fled like sheep and denied Jesus. Their *lack of power* was plainly evident as they hid behind locked doors when Jesus appeared to them and gave them the Holy Spirit.

> So when it was evening on that day, the first {day} of the week, <u>and when the doors were shut where the disciples were, for fear of the Jews</u>, Jesus came and stood in their midst and said to them, 'Peace {be} with you.' John 20:19 (Underline by author.)

By contrast, consider the apostles *after* they received the *Baptism* of the Holy Spirit, a distinctly different event than when the Holy Spirit initially took residence in them. On the

---

[12] Some contend that the original languages of the New Testament were written in Aramaic. In either case, the best known and earliest manuscripts today are written in Greek. Regardless, God has protected His truths.

day of Pentecost, the apostles fearlessly and publicly addressed the same crowd of Jews from whom they had been hiding. This time, however, the disciples had POWER to be His witnesses.

In the coming days, this kind of power is absolutely required for you to stand against the unseen forces of evil even if it means dying as a martyr.

Character alone, although requisite in a Christian's life, does not of itself produce power. If it did, Jesus would NOT have told His disciples to wait in Jerusalem *to receive power*.

Scriptural knowledge, although requisite in a Christian's life, does not of itself produce power. If it did, the apostles would already have been empowered *before* they received the Baptism of the Holy Spirit since Jesus personally taught them over the span of 3.5 years.

Although character and knowledge are important in *maintaining* power, neither one or in combination *produces* power. Power comes from the Holy Spirit's gift—His baptism. Man cannot produce this power of himself.

Again, the *only means* of power Jesus prescribed for His Church comes through the Baptism of the Holy Spirit, or stated in another way, *through the Holy Spirit's gift*.

Based on this truth, consider the contemporary evidence derived from the power of the Baptism of the Holy Spirit since the last century. It is noteworthy that such exploits are NOT *routinely* found in any other aspect of Christianity where the Baptism of the Holy Spirit is denied or refused as relevant for the Church today:

ADVANCEMENTS OF PENTECOST

- In the 1900's after the famous Azusa Street Revival[13], there were relatively very few Pentecostal Christians.

- In 1970 during the Charismatic movement, there were 74 million.

- In 1996, just 26 years later, there were 475 million.

- In 2020 there are an estimated 650 million.

- Pentecostal Christians consistently have the largest evangelistic campaigns in history.

- Pentecostal Christians operate the largest Christian TV/radio programs.

- Pentecostal Christians have the fastest growing number of newly planted churches.

- Pentecostal Christian churches have the fastest rate of membership growth.

- Pentecostal Christians have the largest churches.

- Pentecostal Christians have the most consistent proof of signs, wonders, and miracles.

Without regard to denominational considerations, suffice it to say that those who oppose the Baptism of the Holy Spirit

---

[13] This major revival in Los Angelis launched the 20th century Pentecostal church in America.

do not achieve the same result as compared to those who accept His gift. Both history and contemporary evidence prove this fact.

To be certain, the Endtimes is a season of spiritual and natural powers violently set against one another. In light of that truth, any Christian who rejects the Holy Spirit's gift conversely rejects the spiritual weapons God provides against the supernatural powers of darkness.

This is Our Hour!

As the Church enters her most glorious moment throughout all of time, the signature of her influence will be the fearless power she possesses in Jesus. In the coming days, she will display inarguable evidence marked with mighty signs, wonders, and miracles that leave no doubt as to the proof of God Almighty and His righteousness.

You are marked for such a time in Christ. You have been chosen to be part of an incredible victorious army that cannot be swayed—an army of uncompromising strength to glorify Christ by the testimony you hold, a testimony unto death.[14] Regardless of how severe the trials, His power and presence will be more than enough as He lavishes you with grace upon grace (John 1:16), while moving you from faith to faith (Romans 1:17), and strength to strength (Psalm 84:7).

---

[14] The most dangerous people are those who willingly sacrifice their lives for a higher value. Christians who willingly lay down their lives for Christ are essentially unstoppable except for death.

In **Critical Truth #2,** it is essential to be dressed in power in order to victoriously stand against Satan! While mere flesh is no match against his unquantified power, nonetheless, he fully comprehends when vessels of clay are endued with the Holy Spirit's power. These are the Christians that will take the kingdom by FORCE!

> And from the days of John the Baptist until now the kingdom of heaven suffers violence, and the violent take it by force. Matthew 11:12

CHAPTER 3
CRITICAL TRUTH #3

Three Essential Prophecies

In this Critical Truth, you will discover three key prophecies that were fulfilled in our generation that previous generations did not experience. By the fulfillment of these prophecies, we are positioned for the final steps just before the Book of Revelation opens.

The **first prophecy**, written in 721 BC, foretold the time Israel would again be a sovereign nation after her dissolution for over 2,600 years (Isaiah 11:11).

The **second prophecy**, written in 96 AD foretold the coming of the 7th Beast Empire that arrived 1,852 years later. This is the Beast Empire just before Antichrist's 8th and final Beast Empire (Revelation 17:11).

The **third prophecy**, written in 592 BC, foretold the time Israel would regain sovereign control over the city of Jerusalem after losing it for 2,560 years (Ezekiel 37:1-10). It was said again in Daniel 9:24 (written in 539 BC), that the Jews would be back in possession of Jerusalem after losing it for 2,506 years.

It is amazing that all three prophecies were fulfilled exclusively in our generation. These three prophecies irrefutably confirm, once again, that this generation is the Exit Generation that sees Antichrist's rule over the earth and the coming of the Lord Jesus Christ who destroys him.

1st Prophecy In Our Generation

When Israel turned from the true and living God to pagan idolatry, she departed from the Lord and she lost her sovereign right of governance in her own land. As a result, in 721 BC, God handed her over to Assyria. From that time forward for the next 2,669 years, Israel remained a captive nation. Ultimately, her people were scattered across the globe and blended into various cultures. Nonetheless, there remains an innate identity given to the Jewish people. Regardless of where they live or to the far places they were scattered, they know who they are and from where they came—generation by generation.

According to prophecy, Israel had to become a nation once more within the borders of her same land *before* the 8th Beast Empire of Antichrist's rule could come. In view of that, the **first definitive fulfilled prophecy** that pinpoints our generation was when Israel become a nation again in 1948 AD after 2,669 years of dissolution! This event fulfilled Ezekiel's prophetic vision of the valley of dry bones (Ezekiel 37:3-14) written in 593 BC—over 2,540 years before it was fulfilled. Until this prophecy came to pass, the 8th Beast Empire could not come.

No nation in the history of mankind has ever been disbanded, its people scattered throughout the nations and blended into the cultures for over two millenniums, and then reformed within the borders of their original land.

The Final Scattering of the Jews

On April 7, 32 A.D., Jesus prophesied that the temple would be leveled. In 70 A.D. after Titus' army invaded Jerusalem this prophecy was fulfilled. At that time, his soldiers slaughtered every Jewish man, woman, pregnant woman, and child they could find. Those who survived, fled the land.

During the invasion, Titus' demon-crazed army leveled the temple. From the day of Titus' invasion until 1948 AD, a total of 1,878 years, the Jews remained scattered across the face of the earth!

> When He approached {Jerusalem} [on Sunday, April 6, 32 A. D.] He saw the city and wept over it, 42 saying, "If you had known in this day, even you, the things which make for peace! But now they have been hidden from your eyes. 43 For the days will come upon you [in 70 A.D.] when your enemies will throw up a barricade against you, and surround you and hem you in on every side, 44 and they will level you to the ground and your children within you, and they will not leave in you one stone upon another, <u>because you did not recognize the time of your visitation</u>." Luke 19:41-44 (Square brackets and underline inserted by the author for clarity of context.)

58

> Therefore prophesy and say to them, "Thus says the Lord GOD, Behold, I will open your graves and cause you to come up out of your graves, My people; and I will bring you into the land of Israel." Ezekiel 37:12

After Israel lost her nation, her land was referred to as the Land of Palestine. Then, after WWII, Great Britain relinquished control of Palestine and handed it to the newly formed United Nations.

On Monday, November 29, 1947, the UN passed Resolution 181 that called for a two-state nation of Jews and Arabs. This however, was contrary to God's covenant with Israel that she should be a sovereign nation of the Jews—not a nation having to share her land with another nation.

Approximately seven months later on May 14, 1948, US President Truman sat in the Oval Office of the White House when the subject came up for discussion. After listening to his cabinet members, he got up, walked to his desk, and typed out an official US Proclamation. Then, as an afterthought to his typewritten note, he corrected two original words he had just typed and then hand-wrote the word "Israel" as the new Jewish State. Suddenly, in a single moment, by a single word in our generation and through the President of the United States of America, the prophecy of Ezekiel 37:12 came to pass after more than 2,500 years exactly as God declared!

Accordingly, **the first definitive fulfilled prophecy** pinpoints this generation as the Exit Generation.

2nd Prophecy In Our Generation

Ever since Adam's fall, each succeeding generation has warned that the *end* is near. Such announcements are routinely made on the cusp of every major war, catastrophe, and plague. In 52 A.D., Nero entertained the Roman crowds

This Government has been informed that a Jewish state has been proclaimed in Palestine, and recognition has been requested by the *provisional* Government thereof.

The United States recognizes the provisional government as the de facto authority of the new ~~Jewish state~~ *State of Israel.*

Harry Truman

Approved.
May 14, 1948.

by slaughtering Christians in his coliseums as a spectator event. Accordingly, the Christians of Thessalonica wondered if they had missed the Lord's coming and were divinely handed over to destruction. To set them at ease, the Apostle

Paul sent a letter and explained the chronological order of events that lead to the Rapture.[15]

As previously stated, even though Paul felt the Lord's arrival was soon, more than 1,970 years have passed and still Jesus has not returned.

If Paul knew what signs to look for, how could he, being a premiere apostle, miss the timing of this monumental event by nearly two millenniums? The answer is simple: The Book of Revelation, which contained precisely important facts pertaining to our generation, was not written until 96 A.D., nearly 44 years *after* Paul wrote his letter to the Thessalonians—a full 28 years *after* he was martyred.

In the Book of Revelation, a critically important truth was revealed for the first time. This alarming fact had major influence related to the precise order of the Endtimes: namely that there was yet to come *another* Beast Empire—the 7th, for a total of eight Beast Empires in all.

The 8th Beast Empire is ruled by Antichrist. Only the Book of Revelation speaks of the 7th Beast Empire, an empire of great mystery—that is, until it came into existence.

---

[15] Of the eight Beast Empires, the 8th is headed up by Antichrist who rules the world during the 7-Year Period of Revelation. During his rule, the Rapture occurs. Specifically, Paul's letter in 52 A.D. tells us the sequence of events which points to the time Antichrist will be in office. Paul did not know, however, there would be a total of 8 Beast Empires. Only John mentions the 7th Beast Empire in 96 A.D.—44 years after Paul's letter. Nonetheless, until Paul explained the order, the Thessalonians assumed they were living during the final Beast Empire when in fact they were living during the 6th Beast Empire, the Roman Beast. Yet Paul in no way asserted they were living during the final Beast Empire. In his letter, he instructs them on the order of events leading up to the point of the Rapture.

Even though Daniel's prophecies, written in 538 B.C. reach into our day, they do not reveal the 7th Beast Empire. In fact, the 7th Beast Empire would not be announced until 634 years later when the Apostle John penned the Book of Revelation. Even then, the 7th Beast Empire would not be revealed until 1,849 years later.

Adding more difficulty to the discovery, after John told of it, its identifying markers would not be understood until *after* it had passed. In fact, most readers of Scripture fail to notice the mention of the 7th Beast Empire which is found only in the 17th chapter of Revelation.

> Here is the mind which has wisdom. The seven heads are seven mountains [leaders of the seven Beast Empires] on which the woman [Harlot Babylon] sits, 10 and they are seven kings [leaders of the seven Beast Empires]; five have fallen [Egypt, Assyria, Babylon, Medo-Persia, and Greece], one is [Rome—at the time of John's Revelation], the other [the 7th Beast—Nazi Germany] has not yet come; and when he [Hitler] comes, he must remain a little while [12 years in all]. 11 The Beast which was [a leader of one of the previous seven empires] and is not [because he is still yet to come in the future], is himself also an eighth [Antichrist]

and is one of the seven [leaders of the previous seven empires], and he goes to destruction [when he is killed at the battle of Armageddon]. Revelation 17:9-11 (Square brackets inserted by the author for clarification.)

The 7th Beast Empire is unique because unlike the six previous empires, it is not described by having a national identity. Consequently, it remained nameless and obscure.

Nazi Germany arose under Hitler as the 7th Beast Empire. His was the only official government since the 6th Beast Empire (Rome) that sought the total annihilation of the Jews.

Hitler's reign was very brief, merely 12 years in duration starting from 1933 until 1945. It ended when he committed suicide with a gunshot to his head. Nevertheless, the death toll of 6,000,000 Jews was exceedingly more than any of the previous Beast Empires.

Accordingly, **the second definitive fulfilled prophecy** that pinpoints our generation was the fulfillment of the 7th Beast Empire in 1933 AD. Now that the 7th Beast Empire has come and gone, the stage is set for the final Beast Empire, the 8th, which is ruled by Antichrist.

The death toll connected to the 8th Beast Empire is a staggering ¼ of mankind, or based on today's population, the killing of over 1,975,000,000 people! To put it in relative perspective, it is the combined population of America, Europe, and Africa.

As already mentioned, Paul was martyred in 68 A.D.—28 years *before* the Book of Revelation was penned. For that reason, he never mentions the 7th Beast Empire in any part of his letters to the Thessalonians or Corinthians—the only places he refers to the Rapture.

Had he known of the 7th Beast Empire, he would surely have included it in the order of events leading to Christ's return. And…he would have realized he was living in the era of the 6th Beast Empire of Rome—not the 8th. Regardless of all that, his instructions are completely on point with *this* generation pertaining to the 8th Beast Empire. If anything, the Holy Spirit intended Paul's instructions as having more relevance to our generation than those of the early Church.

3rd Prophecy In Our Generation

Israel had to be in possession and control of Jerusalem which was the next step in the order of fulfilled of prophecy.

Daniel's famous 70-Week Prophecy (Daniel 9:24) said that Jerusalem belongs exclusively to Israel, not the Muslims, the Palestinians, nor any other ethnic or national group of people.

But when Israel became a nation again in 1948, there was still a major problem: she did not have possession of Jerusalem. The city remained under the dominion and control of the Gentles, specifically the Islamic people.

In order for Daniel's key Endtimes prophecies to be fulfilled in their divine order, Jerusalem had to be in possession of the Jews. The fulfillment of this prophecy took place on

Wednesday, June 7, 1967 after a brief war lasting only six days.

> Seventy weeks have been decreed for your people and <u>your</u> Holy City, to finish the transgression, to make an end of sin, to make atonement for iniquity, to bring in everlasting righteousness, to seal up vision and prophecy and to anoint the most holy place. Daniel 9:24 (Underline by author.)

Outnumbered and with little equipment for battle, the 6-Day War Victory against Egypt, Syria, and Jordan was a series of miraculous interventions by the hand of God. Stories abound of God's supernatural works where Israel's enemy soldiers surrendered after seeing vanguards of angels coming to Israel's defense. This proves God's endorsement and favor for the Jews in their land!

Accordingly, **the third fulfilled prophecy** pinpoints our generation as the Exit Generation when the prophecy was completed on June 7, 1967.

No generation but ours saw the fulfillment of these three significant prophecies—prophecies that are directly adjacent to the coming of Antichrist's 8th Beast Empire.

In Critical Truth #3, only our generation is the recipient of these three concisely fulfilled prophecies. This places us at the very threshold for the last remaining events that usher in the 8th Beast Empire. It is important, therefore, that you realize why your generation is the Chosen Generation; that you comprehend that you will see the enthronement of Antichrist in the newly built temple in Jerusalem; and that you know with all certainty you will be rescued by Jesus in an event called "the Rapture of the Saints".

CHAPTER 4
CRITICAL TRUTH #4

The Seven Seals Of Revelation

In this Critical Truth, you will learn about the insights pertaining to the Seals of Revelation. The Seals have the most direct relevance that is critical to our survival. By understanding them, you will know exactly what to do in the coming days based on the precise numbers given in Scripture.

Even though this chapter deals with the Seven Seals, in order to keep things in perspective, I will very briefly deal with the Trumpet and Bowl Judgments that define the Lord's wrath.

The Seals and the Scroll

In the outlay of the Endtimes, the Book of Revelation speaks of Seven Seals, Seven Trumpet Judgments, and Seven Bowl Judgments (see Appendix 2 and 3). All of them are written on a scroll.

Our Heavenly Father possesses the scroll, a rolled parchment with seven seals along the leading edge. Jesus Christ is the only one worthy to break the Seals and unroll the document that releases the judgments of God upon the world.

The timing pertaining to each event is hidden in the Father's wisdom including the exact day Jesus returns at the 6th Seal.

As Jesus breaks each Seal, Satan is permitted to expand his activities on the earth through his ambassador, Antichrist, which includes the time Antichrist strides into the newly built temple in Jerusalem and declares himself to be God. God, however, in His unsearchable wisdom, is setting Satan up for an ultimate bitter destruction.

Paul described all of this as the "Mystery of Iniquity". Even at this moment, the godless masses are unwittingly being prepared to receive Antichrist—the very people who will take his Mark and worship him (II Thessalonians 2:7-10).

The Importance of the Seals

The Seals are merely the conditions that must be met *before* the judgments of God are poured out upon the wicked masses.

However, because of God's great mercy and perfect justice, He will never punish the Righteous with the Wicked. Therefore, the 6th Seal is an event known as the Rapture of the church. This is the moment Jesus returns to earth and calls the Righteous upward to Himself in a "twinkling of an eye"[16]— the speed of less than a blink.[17]

Contrary to the concept of some, we will not float skyward like a feather drifting upward in a thermal of hot air. Rather, it will seem like an instant translation from one place to another.

Those left behind after the Rapture are then subject to the Wrath of God. Therefore, from the moment of the Rapture until the final judgment of God which is the 7th Bowl Judgment, it is a period of time described in Scripture as, "The Day of the Lord".

The Trumpet Judgments on the Wicked

After the last Seal is broken, the Seven Trumpet Judgments commence. Each judgment is initiated by an angel assigned to blow his specific trumpet. In this regard, the trumpet blasts are announcements, each in their proper order, that release cataclysmic events that occur on earth.

The timeframe for the Trumpet Judgments are slightly over 1,260 days in duration from the first to the last. The 5th

---

[16] In Paul's teachings, he uses the phrases, "our gathering together to him" or the "catching away" in II Thessalonians 2:1-3 and II Corinthians 15:51-53. The English word for these events called "Rapture" is not in the literal language of the writings.
[17] I Thessalonians 4:17 speaks of the raptured Saints meeting Him in the clouds.

Trumpet Judgment alone, for instance, is 150 days in duration.[18]

The Bowl Judgments

After the Trumpet Judgments come the Bowl Judgments. They commence within five days of the last trumpet—the 7th Trumpet Judgment. They are described as Bowl Judgments because they are swift and intense as if being "poured out".

The 7th Bowl Judgment

The 7th Bowl Judgment ends with total destruction of all the cities being leveled by a global super-mega-earthquake. Coinciding with that, 100-pound hail stones strike the earth at over 120 mph. This particular earthquake is described in Isaiah 24:19-21 and Revelation 16:18.

The earth is broken apart, the earth is split through, the earth is shaken violently. 20 The earth trembles like a heavy drinker and sways like a hut, for the wrongdoing is heavy upon it, and it will fall, never to rise again. 21 So it will happen on that day, that the Lord will punish the rebellious angels of heaven on high, and the kings of the earth on earth. Isaiah 24:19-21

---

[18] A lunar month, as compared to a solar month, is 30 days long. Revelation is configured along the Lunar Calendar, not the Solar Calendar that we use today.

And there were flashes of lightning and sounds and peals of thunder; and there was a great earthquake, such as there had not been since man came to be upon the earth, so great an earthquake was it, and so mighty. Revelation 16:18

Earthquakes and Tsunamis of Revelation

A super-earthquake as described in Isaiah's prophecy is beyond imagination. Two effects *in combination* follow this particular earthquake—tsunamis and volcanoes.

Currently there are over 1,350 known volcanoes, most of which are dormant. Based on the size of the earthquake during the 7th Bowl Judgment, it can reasonably be expected that a majority of the dormant volcanoes will activate.

To put this particular earthquake in perspective, it will be felt in all land masses throughout the earth. Consequently, super-giant tsunamis traveling over 500 mph will cross the oceans as deep rolling swells.

Characteristic to what tsunamis do, miles from shore, the oceanic swells pull the tidewater toward them while gaining even more mass and power. Then, as the swells continue toward land, the water is pushed upward forming waves. These waves, based upon the size of the earthquake in question, can reasonably be estimated at a 1,000 feet or more in height. Accordingly, between the earthquake and the tsunamis, this judgment wipes out all the islands and levels the mountains. (Isaiah 24:18-23; Revelation 16:18

The Characteristics of Tsunamis

Tsunami (pronounced soo-naa-me) is a Japanese word; 'tsu' meaning harbor and 'nami' meaning wave. A tsunami is a series of huge sea waves typically caused by underwater or costal land disturbances such as earthquakes, landslides, volcanic eruptions, or even from a meteorite collision.

A tsunami comes in a series of waves known as a "wave train". Each wave can be as long as 60 miles (100 kilometers) in latitude and spaced one hour apart in sequence (500 miles apart). The first wave is not necessarily the most destructive.

Such killer waves race across entire oceans while retaining their energy. For instance, the Indian Ocean tsunami on Sunday, December 26, 2004 traveled as far as 3,000 miles (5,000 kilometers) and reached the coastline of eighteen countries: Indonesia, Thailand, India, Sri-Lanka, Malaysia, Myanmar, Bangladesh, Maldives, Reunion Island (French), Seychelles, Madagascar, Mauritius, Somalia, Tanzania, Kenya, Oman, South Africa and Australia.

One of its waves, triggered by an earthquake, was estimated at 100 feet high when it came to shore, and had the energy of 23,000 Hiroshima-type atomic bombs.

"Deep ocean" tsunamis often travel unnoticed at speeds of 500 mph and cross entire bodies of water in less than a day. These result from an *underwater* earthquake on the deep ocean floor.

Depending upon which event causes a tsunami, scientists calculate the arrival times in different parts of the world by using such factors as water depths and distances.

Some tsunamis do not necessarily approach land as breaking waves. Sometimes they masquerade as a very fast rising tide accompanied by subaquatic turbulence that literally suck people and objects underwater in a blender of furious currents. In many such cases, entire beaches are stripped away.

Geologists claim to have found evidence of an historic 1,000-foot high tsunami on the big island of Hawaii. Based on this discovery, it is reasonable to assume that the most severe earthquake since the creation of the world occur during the 7th Bowl Judgment will likely produce a plague of waves ranging from 500 to 1,000 feet all over the world.

Try to imagine the potential of such waves compared to the mere 100-foot wave that hit Indonesia where over 280,000 people were killed. Accordingly, the death and destruction of the tsunami waves during the 7th Bowl Judgment will be unimaginable.

Earthquakes often trigger volcanic activity. An earthquake of this particular caliber will trigger a concert of dormant volcanoes into an active state spewing megatons of ash into the atmosphere and blocking the sunlight.

What Concerns Us Most

That which affects us the most, is the Seals of Revelation. This is where our focus must be centered. By understanding the Seals and the specific timeframes related to them, we will have adequate time to prepare for our escape into the wilderness. Accordingly, the admonitions given by an angel in the book of Daniel refer to our generation.

Those who have insight will shine brightly like the brightness of the expanse of heaven, and those who lead the many to righteousness, like the stars forever and ever. Daniel 12:3

Seals 1-3 and Seals 4-6

With the exception of the 7th Seal, Scripture does not reveal the duration of time for the individual previous six Seals. Rather, the first three Seals stand as one group, and Seals 4 through 6 stand as another group. Scripture reveals that Seals 1 through 3 comprise a timeframe of 1,260 days in duration. By comparison, we do not know the duration for Seals 4 through 6.

If we could know the timeframe of Seals 4 through 6, we could pinpoint the exact day of the Rapture since Jesus comes at the time of the 6th Seal. As previously stated, however, this fact is hidden in the wisdom of our Heavenly Father.

The 7th Seal that lasts about 30-minutes, (Revelation 8:1-2), is designated for the angels to gather who are assigned to the blow the Trumpet Judgments in their exact order. Also, the 7th Seal introduces the coming Trumpet Judgments of God's wrath.

Detailing the Seals

Specifically, in this Critical Truth #4, you will learn the exact signs that precede the opening of the 1st Seal. Accordingly, the timeframes of what you must do to be prepared are based on the precise date that the 1st Seal opens. Further, you will learn what each subsequent Seal means in relative importance to you *right now*. You will also understand what you should be doing *right now* to prepare for this very soon coming event.

By knowing the exact number of days from Seal 1 through Seal 3, which is 1,260 days in duration, you can precisely know the day the 4th Seal opens. This is when the Mark of the Beast is required of all people along with the command to worship the image of Antichrist.

The time between the 3rd Seal and the 4th Seal is perhaps less than a day where major events occur as will be explained in this chapter.

Then, between the 4th Seal and the 6th Seal, you must prepare for what Jesus said would be the most troubling time the world has ever known and will never occur again (Matthew 24:21-22).

But take heart! The power and presence of the Lord will be with each Christian. He will add grace upon grace, strength upon strength, and faith upon faith. Through Him, we are more than conquerors!

"For then there will be a great tribulation, such as has not occurred since the beginning of the world until now, nor ever will. 22 "Unless those days had been cut short, no life would have been saved; but for the sake of the elect those days will be cut short. 23 "Then if anyone says to you, 'Behold, here

is the Christ,' or 'There *He is*,' do not believe *him.* 24 "For false Christs and false prophets will arise and will show great signs and wonders, so as to mislead, if possible, even the elect. 25 "Behold, I have told you in advance. 26 "So if they say to you, 'Behold, He is in the wilderness,' do not go out, *or,* 'Behold, He is in the inner rooms,' do not believe *them.* 27 "For just as the lightning comes from the east and flashes even to the west, so will the coming of the Son of Man be. 28 "Wherever the corpse is, there the vultures will gather.
Matthew 24:21-28

Indisputable Signs "Leading" to the 1ˢᵗ Seal

Before Jesus opens the 1ˢᵗ Seal, there will be a great war with Israel (this is detailed in Chapter 6). This particular war will impact world energy prices and by consequence, affect everyone.

As the war develops, the increasing size of military forces against Israel will become so overwhelming that she knows her destruction is absolute. When this happens, she will entreat to the nations for help. Based upon the urgency of her plea, a leader will come forth representing a 3-Nation Coalition and offer her a 7-Year Peace Pact (Daniel 9:27).

Her acceptance of this offer will be a fatal mistake for relying upon the arm of man instead of calling on the Lord. The person leading this 3-Nation Coalition is none other than Antichrist. Moreover, his covenant of peace is actually a covenant with death.

When the Peace Pact is signed, the moment the pen lifts from the paper, the 1st Seal of Revelation opens. THIS IS A CRITICAL EVENT! It starts the countdown of your 1,260-Day Period. Pay close attention to the countdown! Accuracy is vital for your survival.

> Because you have said, "We have made a covenant with death, and with Sheol we have made a pact. The overwhelming scourge will not reach us when it passes by, for we have made falsehood our refuge and we have concealed ourselves with deception." Isaiah 28:15

Christians *will be present on the earth during the first three Seals*! Whatever you do, do not believe the fallacious doctrine of those who tell you otherwise. Those who describe themselves as "Pre-Tribulationists" ardently believe that the Rapture will happen *before* the 1st Seal

There is *nothing* in Scripture to support their claim that the Rapture occurs *before* the 1st Seal is opened. Such erroneous assertions are based purely on logic along with various philosophical assumptions by using out-of-context verses in the Bible, primarily that of I Thessalonians 5:9.

For God has not destined us [the Christians] for wrath [which He will pour out on the wicked], but for obtaining salvation through our Lord Jesus Christ, I Thessalonians 5:9 (Square brackets inserted by the author for clarification.)

The misapplication of the above verse is based on the assumption that the Seals are God's judgments when in fact they are the conditions that must be met "before" God's judgments begin. Consequently, this Scripture DOES NOT apply to the Tribulation against the Saints that starts from the 4th Seal and goes through the 6th Seal. This time period is exclusively the work of Antichrist, not God.

Those asserting that the Rapture occurs "before" the 1st Seal are the very Christians who are completely unprepared when the Mark of the Beast is imposed upon the world. Their fallacious doctrine fails to distinguish between the works of Antichrist upon the Saints as distinguished from God's wrath upon the Wicked.

But make no mistake about it, the Christian is not destined for God's wrath. Therefore, the fundamental purpose of the Rapture is to remove the Saints from the earth before the judgments begin at the time of the 6th Seal just before God pours out His fury.

✸1st Seal ✸

MAN OF PEACE—WHITE HORSE

Then I saw when the Lamb broke one of the seven seals, and I heard one of the four living creatures saying as with a voice of thunder, "Come." 2 I looked, and behold, a white horse, and he who sat on it had a bow; and a crown was given to him, and he went out conquering and to conquer. Revelation 6:1-2

In Revelation, there are two different riders on two different white horses. We must realize that the rider on the white horse associated with the 1st Seal is NOT Jesus Christ, but rather Antichrist. Later in the chronology of Revelation at the time of the 7th Bowl Judgment, specifically at the Battle of Armageddon, Jesus is also depicted as a rider on a white horse as noted below:

And I saw Heaven opened, and behold, a white horse, and He [Jesus Christ] who sat on it is called Faithful and True, and in righteousness He judges and wages war. Revelation 19:11 (Square brackets inserted by the author for clarity of context.)

The rider on the white horse of the "1st Seal" is Antichrist who offers Israel the 7-Year Peace Pact. He is described as having a crown, a bow, no arrow, and his strategy is to conquer by fronting a deceitful impression of peace. Using this facade, he will prove to be the greatest killer of mankind throughout all humanity.

Watch for the war as a precursor leading to the 1st Seal which is the same war where Antichrist offers Israel a Peace Pact. Accordingly, the signing of the 7-Year Peace Pact is the critical event that starts the clock for the next 1,260 days ending with the completion of the 3rd Seal.

The White Horse Persona

Antichrist maintains the false impression of his "white horse persona" to the world through the first three seals. In this manner, he stages himself before the world as a skilled and benevolent leader who can solve the problems of global unrest. By using his vast military strength comprised of ten nations, he is able to bring contentious nations under control. Accordingly, the 2nd Seal represents his mega-military power of the red horse which is Wars and Rumors of Wars.

✸2nd Seal✸

WARS—RED HORSE

When He broke the second seal, I heard the second living creature saying, "Come." 4 And another, a red horse, went out; and to him who sat on it, it was granted to take peace from the earth, and that {men} would slay one another; and a great sword was given to him. Revelation 6:3-4.

You will be hearing of wars and rumors of wars. See that you are not frightened, for {those things} must take place, but {that} is not yet the end. Matthew 24:6

In the 2nd Seal, wars and rumors of war proliferate among nations over energy, economics, religion, and food issues. In the process of Antichrist's transitions, Israel will bask in what they think is *peace* under the guardianship of his 3-Nation Coalition. What she does not suspect is that he is setting her up for destruction.

Additionally, by the time the 2nd Seal opens, Antichrist will have amassed a 10-Nation Confederation[19] that can easily be identified. Concerning this 10-Nation Confederation (which includes his original 3-Nation Coalition), look for their combined political, economic, and military power. It will be unlike any person in the history of the world has ever achieved.

Factious nations will be forced to comply with Antichrist's global mandates by various means. This will serve to enhance his reputation throughout the world that he is a genius of a leader. In fact, on a global scale, he will possess such

---

[19] This is not the current European Economic Community of nations whose changing membership is unpredictable.

great power and influence that according to Revelation 13:4, the populace of the world will say:

Who is like the Beast, and who is able to wage war with him?

During the 2nd Seal, Antichrist moves from the staging ground of Israel's Peace Pact and enlarges his global influence. His armies will become the new *peacekeeping* forces. Added to that, the United Nations will most certainly submit to his control and gladly mingle their troops with his. Even more, their UN policies will be fully matched with his agenda. Consequently, the Jews will not be the only ones who claim Antichrist is the answer, but eventually the whole world.

Antichrist's plan, as previously stated in the 1st Seal, is to conquer by the means of false peace. Israel will NOT suspect him as a violent man, but as one who is their friend. In that regard, Scripture issues a sober warning to Israel and even the whole world:

> While they are saying, "Peace and safety!" then destruction will come upon them suddenly like labor pains upon a woman with child, and they will not escape. I Thessalonians 5:3

Obviously, Antichrist's powers and intelligence come from Satan. During the first three Seals, Antichrist does nothing to discredit himself. If his true character were revealed prior to the 3rd Seal, Israel would most certainly be suspicious of his protection. In consideration of that, the imagery of the red horse (2nd Seal) and the black horse (3rd Seal) is largely the unseen works of Satan who sends his demonic minions throughout the world to create havoc while at the same time presenting Antichrist's "white horse diplomacy" as the answer.

✸3rd Seal✸

FEEDER OF MEN—BLACK HORSE

When He broke the third seal, I heard the third living creature saying, "Come." I looked, and behold, a black horse; and he who sat on it had a pair of scales in his hand. 6 And I heard {something} like a voice in the center of the four living creatures saying, "A quart of wheat for a denarius, and three quarts of barley for a denarius; and do not damage the oil and the wine." Revelation 6:5-6 (Underline by author.)

For nation will rise against nation, and kingdom against kingdom, and in various places there will be famines and earthquakes. Matthew 24:6-7 (Underline by author.)

The consequence of wars and earthquakes is famine, and with earthquakes come tsunamis. Title waves will be more widespread, larger in size, and immensely more destructive along the coastal regions of the world as the severity and frequency of earthquakes increase.

> **For we know that the whole creation groans and suffers the pains of childbirth together until now.** Romans 8:22

Massive population groups will be devastated, leaving multiple thousands without food. Fertile coastal fields will either be destroyed or left untended for the lack of laborers or the lack of farming equipment. Such population groups will look to the wealth and power of Antichrist's 10-Nation Confederation as the only one who can help them.

It is unlikely that the famines connected to the 2nd and 3rd Seal are global. Most likely, the famines will be localized to war-torn zones and natural disaster areas. Meanwhile, Antichrist will seize the opportunity to gain more popularity by sending his military forces onto the scene with food, shelter, and medical relief. For this reason, the world will see him as a caring compassionate leader.

Very likely, his increasing economic wealth which is achieved from the collective of his 10-Nation Confederation will shape the food markets and its related costs. Accordingly, Scripture indicates that Antichrist will sell food supplies from his mega-economic controls. It will cost the consumer a full day's wage to purchase a mere ⅛ of the quantity normally purchased at regular prices. After all, anyone who controls the food, controls the people.

Overview of Seals 1 Through 3

Again, keep this important fact in mind: Seals 1 through 3 are the staging-ground opportunities for Antichrist to gain world endorsement. This is NOT the time of the Tribulation. But by using false peace as a strategy, he will successfully disarm suspicion among the global masses and enlist their favor.

The well informed Christian should be watching for a world leader that heads up a 3-Nation Coalition. Doubtless, the political events surrounding this acquisition will be well publicized in the international media systems. The key, however, is to recognize the methods of such acquisition. Will it be by the conquest of one nation taking over another, or perhaps by economics? Whatever is the means, the end result will the combined strength of three nations acting as one under the headship of Antichrist.

By the time the first three Seals are finished, Antichrist will have gained world recognition as a political and military genius.

Going back to the 3rd Seal, by the time it ends, 1,260 days will have elapsed since the signing of the 7-Year Peace Pact with Israel.

The preparations you *should have been doing* "during" the 1,260-Day Period from Seals 1 through 3 is covered in the Critical Truth #5 following the explanation of the Seals.

It is vitally important that you start preparing NOW at the time of this reading. There are practical things you need to study and skills you need to develop such as how to build an enduring functional shelter; how to build a root cellar; how to purify water; and how to keep food from spoiling, to name just a few.

By the time Antichrist invades Jerusalem, it will be too late to acquire the necessary skills and equipment. For this reason, the combined strengths, skills, and knowledge of a "team" is better than an individual.

Between Seals 3 and 4

Accordingly, *after* the 3rd Seal ends, but *before* the 4th Seal begins, Antichrist's true intensions are revealed when he breaks covenant with Israel's 7-Year Peace Pact. This is the time he suddenly moves against Israel with his military and takes over the newly built temple in Jerusalem. Once that is accomplished, he declares himself as God—an event Jesus referred to in Daniel's prophecy (Matthew 24:15) as, "The Abomination of Desolation". Accordingly, between the 3rd and 4th Seal is a juncture of major events, including the issuing of a command by the False Prophet to receive the Mark of the Beast and worship Antichrist. This is the "Midpoint" of the 7-Year Period, and yes, the Christians will be on earth at this time.

The 4th Seal commences the very next day with the enforcement of the command for everyone to receive the Mark and make an image of Antichrist to worship it. This is the starting point of the Tribulation—a global slaughter of all who refuse to worship him. It begins in Jerusalem.

The False Prophet has the same power and authority as Antichrist, but his role is distinguished as a spiritual support for him. Of no surprise, he is as evil and diabolical as Antichrist.

Anyone who receives the Mark of the Beast and worships Antichrist commits an unpardonable sin and they are sealed unto eternal damnation. Those who accept the Mark only live another 1,335 days under Antichrist's collapsing kingdom while faced with the destructive judgments of God before they are cast into hell.

As an act of mercy and justice, God sends an angel that super-sonically travels the world warning its inhabitants NOT to take the Mark or worship the image.

> Then another angel, a third one, followed them, saying with a loud voice, "If anyone worships the Beast and his image, and receives a mark on his forehead or on his hand, 10 he also will drink of the wine of the wrath of God, which is mixed in full strength in the cup of His anger; and he will be tormented with fire and brimstone in the presence of the holy angels and in the presence

of the Lamb. 11 And the smoke of their torment goes up forever and ever; they have
no rest day and night, those who worship
the Beast and his image, and whoever receives the mark of his name." Revelation 14:9-11

The Two Heavenly Prophets

Between the 3rd and 4th Seal, God sends two prophets from
Heaven, Enoch and Elijah. They are the only two men recorded in Scripture who have been taken into Heaven without
dying and kept by God for this time.

Enoch walked with God so closely, that God took him
(Genesis 5:21-24) and Elijah was taken to Heaven in a chariot
of fire (II Kings 2:11). Since that time, they have been referred to in Zechariah 4:11 and have been reserved for such a
time as this.

Enoch represents the Gentile race of people while Elijah
represents the Jewish race of people. They return to earth and
prophesy for 1,260 days[20] starting from the 4th Seal until they
are martyred at the time of the 6th Trumpet Judgment.

During the appointed time of their 1,260 days of ministry,
they strike the earth with judgments as often as they wish and
are invincible. If anyone tries to harm them, by the very words
issued from their mouths their assailants are killed.

---

[20] This is the second set of 1,260 days not to be confused with the first set of 1,260
days assigned to Seal 1-3.

And I will grant {authority} to my two witnesses, and they will prophesy for twelve hundred and sixty days **[3.5 lunar years starting from the Midpoint of the 7-Year Period of Revelation]**, clothed in sackcloth. 4 These are the two olive trees and the two lampstands that stand before the Lord of the earth. 5 And if anyone wants to harm them, fire **[authority and judgment]** flows out of their mouth and devours their enemies; so if anyone wants to harm them, he must be killed in this way [by their words that bring instant judgment]. 6 These have the power to shut up the sky, so that rain will not fall during the days of their prophesying; and they have power over the waters to turn them into blood, and to strike the earth with every plague, as often as they desire. 7 When they have finished their testimony, the Beast **[Antichrist]** that comes up out of the Abyss will make war with them, and overcome them and kill them. 8 And their dead bodies {will lie} in the street of the great city which mystically is called Sodom and Egypt, where also their Lord was crucified. Revelation 11:3-8 (Square brackets and underline inserted by the author for clarity of context.)

✹4ᵗʰ through 6ᵗʰ Seals✹
The Tribulation Period

Seals 4 through 6 is the time known as the Tribulation. It commences when the 4ᵗʰ Seal opens and continues until Jesus comes at the time of the 6ᵗʰ Seal to Rapture the Saints. Jesus said of this time:

> For then there will be a <u>great tribulation</u>, such as has not occurred since the beginning of the world until now, nor ever will. 22 Unless those days had been cut short, no life would have been saved; but for the sake of the Elect **[those who remain true to Jesus]** those days will be cut short. Matthew 24:21-22
> (Square brackets and underline inserted by the author for clarity of context.)

A World Caught Unaware

Where are the Christians during the Tribulation from Seals 4 through 6? Is there any ministry sharing Christ, either by radio, TV, or published written material? Where are the churches and who is filling them?

The answer is obvious: After Antichrist declares himself as God, all religious venerations are forbidden except the worship of him only. This includes all Catholic, Protestant, Buddhist, Islam, and all forms of indigenous native religions.

The Harlot Babylon system, which is comprised of the world's religious and economic enterprises mentioned in Scripture, are destroyed and its resources transferred to the exclusive control of Antichrist (Revelation 18:1-3).

Today, many Christians are ignorant, disinterested, or have been taught fallacious doctrines concerning the End-times. As a result, they will be caught unaware and without preparation when the pivotal moment comes. Such unprepared Christians, taken by surprise, will ardently refuse Antichrist's order to worship him. This is partly the reason why the death toll is so enormous at over 1,975,000,000 people.[21]

Antichrist will kill over 2,700,000 Christians a day during his scourge throughout the earth, a number equal to about 75,000 people an hour. The only thing that stops him from killing all the Righteous people is the coming of the Lord during the 6th Seal.

Meanwhile, the solitary voices speaking for God, beginning from the 4th Seal, are the two invincible prophets from Heaven that forecast the coming judgments of God before they happen.[22] Not even Antichrist can stop the prophets until they have finished their appointed time which is another set of 1,260 days ending at the 6th Trumpet Judgment.

---

[21] This is currently ¼ of mankind based on the 2020 censes of 7,850,000,000 people currently on the earth.

[22] A common untrue assumption is that the 144,000 Jews who are the Firstfruits of Israel will be out evangelizing the world. This is completely unsupported anywhere in Scripture.

✵5th Seal✵

The Martyred Saints Cry Out

By the time the 5th Seal opens, Antichrist's global massacre is well under way to rid the earth of all godly people, and a vast number of the Saints will have been martyred. From their position in Heaven, they cry out to God and ask how much longer before He avenges their blood upon the wicked inhabitants on the earth.

The number of Saints that are martyred by this time is impossible to estimate, but the chorus of their prayers will be counted in the millions upon millions.

> When the Lamb broke the fifth seal, I saw underneath the altar the souls of those who had been slain because of the Word of God, and because of the testimony which they had maintained; 10 and they cried out with a loud voice, saying, "How long, O Lord, holy and true, will You refrain from judging and avenging our blood on those who dwell on the earth?" 11 And there was given to each of them a white robe; and they were told that they should rest for a little while longer, until {the number of} their fellow servants and their brethren who were to be killed even as they had been, would be completed also.
> Revelation 6:9-11

Their prayers are memorialized as a living testament which are answered at the close of the 7th Seal just before God pours out His judgments.

> Then another angel [the angel of the 7th Seal], who had a golden censer, came and stood at the altar. He was given much incense to offer, <u>along with the prayers of all the saints</u>, on the golden altar before the throne. 4 And the smoke of the incense, together with the prayers of the saints rose up before God from the hand of the angel. 5 Then the angel took the censer, filled it with fire from the altar, and hurled it to the earth; and there were peals of thunder, and rumblings, and flashes of lightning, and an earthquake....Revelation 8:3-5. (Underline by author.)

✸6th Seal✸

The Coming of the Lord

Scripture is very specific that no man knows the day or hour of the Lord's return for His people. This means no one is allowed to know when He comes. And yet, there are some today who foolishly and vainly ignore this fact that leads many ill-informed naive Christians astray by their ridiculous claims.

But of that day or hour no one knows, not even the angels in heaven, nor the Son [before His reglorification], but the Father {alone.} Mark 13:32

Behold, He is coming with the clouds, and every eye will see Him, even those who pierced Him; and all the tribes of the earth will mourn over Him. So it is to be. Amen. Revelation 1:7

For just as the lightning comes from the east and flashes even to the west, so will the coming of the Son of Man be. Matthew 24:27

For you yourselves know full well that the day of the Lord will come just like a thief in the night. 3 While they [the naive, unsuspecting, and unbelievers] are saying, "Peace and safety!" then destruction will come upon them suddenly like labor pains upon a woman with child, and they will not escape. I Thessalonians 5:2-3 (Square brackets inserted by the author for clarification.)

There will be signs in sun and moon and stars, and on the earth dismay among nations, in perplexity at the roaring of the sea and the waves, 26 men fainting from fear and the expectation of the things [specifically the impending judgments of God] which are coming upon the world; for the powers of the heavens will be shaken. 27 Then they will see THE SON OF MAN COMING IN A CLOUD with power and great glory. 28 But when these things begin to take place, straighten up and lift up your heads, because your redemption [the Rapture] is drawing near. Luke 21:25-28 (Square brackets inserted by the author for clarity of context.)

Antichrist's Killing Methods During the Tribulation

Antichrist kills by four means: (1) sword: military; (2) pestilence: toxic chemical spraying of communities; (3) famine: starvation by those rounded up and placed in detainment camps; and (4) by the demonic reporting voices coming from the beast images that order the death of those who refuse to take the Mark of the Beast.

To survive Antichrist's global scourge, the only instruction given by Jesus is to be in hiding "before" the Mark of the Beast is commanded upon all people. You must be completely off the grid and visible to no one. Whoever is discovered, will be captured and killed (Matthew 24:16).

Seek and Destroy Technology

Today, there are over 5,300 satellites in space equipped with amazing technology. For instance, when a spy satellite passes over the house of a person, it can detect if the washing machine is operating, or if the TV is on, or any number of operations in the home including voice conversations.

Spy satellites can zoom in close enough to see a two-inch resolution such as the dimples on a golf ball, or people sitting on a park bench while reading, or the details on a person's clothes.

Military personnel who are sitting at a desk thousands of miles away can send a missile from a drone in the sky with pinpoint accuracy through satellite imagery.

1st World Nations such as the USA, Canada, and other European nations currently possess such technology within their military inventory to monitor populations. But 3rd World nations and those less equipped with such technology would rely on the technology of better endowed nations to assist in locating hidden pockets of people fleeing from Antichrist.

But With the Lord's Covering...

As we flee to the wilderness, we should confidently expect the Lord's covering against the works of technology. One of God's protections, therefore, is to keep His people hidden. At the same time, let us not be presumptuous by assuming to walk about in plain view of Antichrist's disciples without consequences.

Again, the only directive Jesus gave to survive the Tribulation was to flee to the wilderness. What you do NOW in preparation for Antichrist's global scourge will determine if you and your loved ones are either martyred, or if you survive the Tribulation until Jesus comes.

Orphan Children of Christians

While the Scriptures do not specifically say what becomes of children that are bereft of their parents that Antichrist kills, it is not an unreasonable assumption that such children will be fostered into the homes of Antichrist's disciples and given the Mark of the Beast.

But remember, the penalty for taking the Mark of the Beast only applies to those who receive it willfully. This means if it is forced upon people, particularly those in captivity, there is no consequence to those having the Mark. Further, those who are incapable of moral understanding would be exempt from guilt as well. This is deduction is based upon the consistency of various principles found in Scripture. But again, this particular situation is not addressed in the Bible.

When Jesus Comes for His Saints

As previously stated, from the 4th Seal onward to the 6th Trumpet Judgment, the two prophets from Heaven will be telling the world of God's coming judgments before they occur. Their words will be ominous warnings to those who have not yet received the Mark of the Beast by telling them that they should worship only God; that Jesus is returning for His Saints; and that when the Lord comes, He is coming with unquenchable fury.

Because their words are infallible with perfect accuracy, the media systems will broadcast their prophecies while lifting up Antichrist as the world's venerated hero. But when Jesus comes for His Saints, exactly as the two prophets foretold, suddenly a sobering fearful moment arrives. For those who took the Mark of the Beast, it is too late. They know God's fury will be released on the same day that Jesus appears for His Saints and removes them by means of the Rapture.

Wherever the Christian is, they will know it is THE day of the Lord's coming based on six signs listed in Matthew 24:29-31 and Revelation 6:12-17. I'll detail those six signs, but first read the Scriptures that speaks of His coming:

> For the Lord Himself will descend from heaven with a shout, with the voice of {the} archangel and with the trumpet of God, and the dead in Christ will rise first. 17 Then we who are alive and remain will be caught up together with them in the clouds to meet the Lord in the air, and so we shall always be with the Lord. I Thessalonians 4:16-17

Behold, I show you a mystery; we shall not all sleep [die], but we shall all be changed, 52 In a moment, in the twinkling of an eye, at the last trump [the last sound of the trumpet, not the last trumpet judgment]: for the trumpet shall sound, and the dead shall be raised incorruptible, and we

shall be changed. II Corinthians 15:51-52 (KJV) (Square brackets and underline inserted by the author for clarity of context.)

> Then they will see THE SON OF MAN COMING IN CLOUDS with great power and glory. 27 And then He will send forth the angels, and will gather together His Elect from the four winds, from the farthest end of the earth to the farthest end of heaven. Mark 13:26-27

On the Day of His Return

On the day Jesus comes to Rapture His Righteous ones, six signs precede His arrival:

1. A great earthquake: every island and mountain are moved out of their place.

2. The sun will be turned black as sackcloth.

3. The moon will be blood red.

4. The stars will fall from the sky (possibly a meteorite shower).

5. The sky will peel back like a scroll and they will see Jesus coming in the clouds.

6. The "Rapture Trumpet" sounds and then suddenly we are gone in less than the time of a blink.

There will be signs in sun and moon and stars, and on the earth dismay among nations, in perplexity at the roaring of the sea and the waves, 26 men fainting from fear and the expectation of the things which are coming upon the world; for the powers of the heavens will be shaken. 27 Then they will see THE SON OF MAN COMING IN A CLOUD with power and great glory. 28 <u>But when these things begin to take place, straighten up and lift up your heads, because your redemption is drawing near</u>. Luke 21:25-28 (Underline by author.)

When Jesus comes in full glorious disclosure, it is a terrifying moment for the wicked masses. From this point forward, God pours forth His wrath. Suddenly, Antichrist is displayed before the entire world as completely helpless. Their venerated hero is now a pitiful helpless loser.

Even though the godless masses quickly realize that he is <u>not</u> God Almighty, they are nonetheless given over to deception. Added to this, the words of the two prophets will be crystal clear about God's coming wrath that sends the world into total panic:

And they [the wicked ones] said to the mountains and to the rocks, 'Fall on us and hide us from the presence of Him who sits on the throne, and from the wrath of the

Lamb; 17 for the great day of their wrath has come **[meaning it has finally come]**, and who is able to stand?' Revelation 6:16-17 (Square brackets inserted by the author for clarity of context.)

What's Next?

While the earth panics in fear, there is a celebration in Heaven with all the Saints who have received their glorified bodies. These are the very ones who came through the Tribulation. This also includes ALL the Saints from the time of Adam, those killed by Antichrist, and those who survived the Tribulation. Accordingly, on the same day Jesus removes His Saints off the earth, the 7th Seal, which lasts only 30 minutes, immediately opens. This is the moment when the prayers of the Saints from under the altar of the 5th Seal are remembered.

✹7th Seal✹

Prayers of the Martyred Are Answered

When the 7th Seal is broken, an angel with a golden censor filled with the prayers of the Saints is hurled to the earth resulting in thunder, rumblings, lightening, and an earthquake. This is also the time that the seven angels who are assigned to blow the Trumpet Judgments are assembled.

In view of those events, the 6th Seal, 7th Seal, and 1st Trumpet Judgment all happen on the same day. Basically, as the Saints go up, the wrath of God comes down.

101

Then another angel, who had a golden censer, came and stood at the altar. He was given much incense to offer, along with the prayers of all the saints, on the golden altar before the throne. 4 And the smoke of the incense, together with the prayers of the saints rose up before God from the hand of the angel. 5 Then the angel took the censer, filled it with fire from the altar, and hurled it to the earth; and there were peals of thunder, and rumblings, and flashes of lightning, and an earthquake. Revelation 8:3-5

In Heaven, a Great Celebration

After these things I looked, and behold, a great multitude which no one could count, from every nation and {all} tribes and peoples and tongues, standing before the throne and before the Lamb, clothed in white robes, and palm branches {were} in their hands; 10 and they cry out with a loud voice, saying, "Salvation to our God who sits on the throne, and to the Lamb." 11 And all the angels were standing around the throne and {around} the elders and the four living creatures; and they fell on their faces before the throne and worshiped God, 12 saying, "Amen, blessing and glory and wisdom and thanksgiving and honor and power and might, {be} to our God forever and ever. Amen." 13 Then one of the elders answered, saying to me, "These who are clothed in the white robes, who are they, and where have they come from?" 14 I said to him, "My lord, you know." And he said to me, <u>"These are the ones who come out of the great tribulation</u>, and they have washed their robes and made them white in the blood of the Lamb. 15 For this reason, they are before the throne of God; and they serve Him day and night in His temple; and He who sits on the throne will spread His tabernacle over them. 16

They will hunger no longer, nor thirst any-more; nor will the sun beat down on them, nor any heat; 17 for the Lamb in the center of the throne will be their shepherd, and will guide them to springs of the water of life; and God will wipe every tear from their eyes." Revelation 7:9-17 (Underline by author.)

In this Critical Truth #4, you must know the details of the Seven Seals and how they relate to current events. Be watching for the great war with Israel and the signing of the 7-Year Peace Pact. This starts the countdown for the 1,260-Day Period that enables you to know when to flee to your refuge. PREPARATION TIME IS NOW.

CHAPTER 5
CRITICAL TRUTH #5

Who Is Antichrist?

In this Critical Truth #5, you will learn the precise identity of Antichrist. Needless to say, he stands in a class all his own as the most fiendish evil man throughout all of humanity.

Initially, his identity will be revealed as the leader of a 3-Nation Coalition that grows into a 10-Nation Confederation. He is further affirmed when he settles a global conflict with Israel and offers her a 7-Year Peace Pact. Before that, however, you will know his exact identity by the evidence of indisputable prophecy. Despite such evidence, many find it challenging to believe.

Foolish Attempts

Down through the years, people have erroneously purported Antichrist's identity in an ever-changing list of well-known people such as Henry Kissinger, Barack Obama, Donald Trump, or even leaders from various Islamic nations. In every case, they have been wrong.

In the blossom of pride, others have resorted to hidden esoteric riddles and puzzles by using flamboyant claims based on ridiculous notions and portraying themselves as master riddle solvers.

> Wisdom is needed here. Let the one with understanding solve the meaning of the number of the beast, for it is the number of a man. His number is 666. Revelation 13:18

Aside from all the foolish proposals concerning Antichrist's identity, the only undeniable evidence comes through Bible prophecy.

What follows is an amazing 4-way intersection of prophetic detail, all standing in concert that are interrelated one to the other. These are the only reliable proofs that definitively identify him.

Even by knowing these prophecies, Antichrist's identity is challenging for some to accept because it conflicts with their pre-disposed presumptions of Scripture. For this, I refer the reader to the **"three overlapping precautions"** of Scriptural contemplation that was shared in the Introduction.

Four Identifying Markers of Antichrist

To properly identify Antichrist, there are four markers that apply exclusively to him and no other. It is difficult to present them individually because they are interconnected and codependent. Nonetheless, the four are listed as follows: (1) His lineage, (2) His leadership, (3) His death, and (4) His miraculous origin.

First Clue…His Lineage

To give adequate contextual understanding concerning his lineage, Noah's three sons, Shem, Japheth, and Ham, must be considered.

After the flood when Noah's family came off the ark, the Lord commanded them to subdue and replenish the earth. Instead, for 300 years, they stayed in the plains of Shinar. They were all of one language and grew into a great population. If you recall, this begins the time of the 4th Cycle of Evil as explained in Chapter 1.

After God scattered the people and confounded their language, Shem's people traveled east forming the Semitic people.

Japheth's people traveled north across the Caucasus Mountains and filled up Europe.

Ham's people traveled south to Africa and India.

The person of most interest is Japheth, specifically, his second son, Magog. By the time God scattered the people, Magog was a prince. He took his group northward, and grew as a massive people until all of Europe was comprised of his lineage.

Various Names of Antichrist

Throughout Scripture, various names have been assigned to Antichrist. In fact, Antichrist is not a man's name, but a description of the leader of the 8th Beast Empire who stands against Christ. Consider, therefore, his names and pay special attention to "Gog".

GOG...Ezekiel 38:2

ANTICHRIST......................................I John 2:18

THE BEAST.....................................Revelation 13:4

THE MAN OF LAWLESSNESS...II Thessalonians 2:3

THE SON OF DESTRUCTION... .II Thessalonians 2:3

POWERFUL UNGODLY KING............Daniel 11:36

THE LITTLE HORN..............................Daniel 7:8

THE DESTROYER AND EXTORTIONER..Isaiah 16:4

HEAD OF THE HOUSE OF EVIL...... .Habakkuk 3:13

ABOMINATION OF DESOLATION.....Matthew 24:15

Gog, the Chief Prince

Of all Antichrist's titles, Gog, his ancient Old Testament name, is the only one that reveals his lineage. This is an important key that unlocks his identity.

Son of man, set thy face against Gog, the land of Magog, the chief prince of Meshech and Tubal [western Russia], and prophesy against him...Ezekiel 38:2 (Square brackets inserted by the author for clarity of context.)

Based on the above verse, Gog is a chief prince in the land of Magog, specifically, from the lineage of Magog. Accordingly, Antichrist's lineage is Magogic. This vital clue is an important piece of evidence employed in the elimination process pertaining to the seven choices of leaders given in Scripture for us to consider.

Second Clue...His Death

I'll briefly touch upon Antichrist's death and then expound on how this relates to his previous leadership roles. Suffice it for now to focus on the cause of his death.

> I saw that one of the heads of the beast seemed wounded beyond recovery—but the fatal wound was healed! The whole world marveled at this miracle and gave allegiance to the beast. Revelation 13:3

To explain this, John was shown a beast having seven heads and ten horns. One of the seven heads had a headwound that was seemingly beyond recovery.

The seven heads represent the seven leaders of the previous seven Beast Empires: Egypt, Assyria, Babylon, Medo-Persia, Greece, Rome, Nazi Germany.

The ten horns act in concert together and represent Antichrist's 10-Nation Confederation through which he rules the world as the leader of the 8th Beast Empire. Conversely, the

109

8th Beast Empire is comprised of ten nations under Antichrist's control.

Regarding the manner of his death, initially we logically assume he will be assassinated *during* his rule of the 8th Beast Empire. As rational as that sounds concerning his fatal headwound, it is not true. A close examination of Scripture refutes that idea.

Scripture is very plain in its language that *before* Antichrist takes his position in the 8th Beast Empire, he would have *first* been a leader of one of the seven *previous* Beast Empires. Consequently, during his prior rule as one of the seven leaders, he died from a fatal headwound. Difficult as this may be for some people to understand, at some point in our generation, he has already been brought back to life and is now a fully functional man.

It is important to remember as a matter of perspective that in our generation, the seven previous Beast Empires are all historic. But, the 10-Nation Confederation is yet to come in the very near future.

Third Clue...His Leadership Roles

The third clue regards Antichrist's roll in one of the seven previous Beast Empires. As previously stated, the Book of Revelation was given to John in 96 AD. when he was exiled to the Island of Patmos by the Roman government—the 6th Beast Empire.

In the 17th chapter of Revelation, the 7th Beast Empire is mentioned for the first and only time in the Bible. Its description is so subtle and demure it is easily missed. For unlike the previous six beast empires that have a national identity, the 7th is described by the personal pronoun "he".

Below is the 17th Chapter of Revelation from verses 7 through 14. Square brackets are inserted to explain the context of the verses and their application. Read it slowly. The compression of information in this chapter is astounding:

And the angel said to me [John], "Why do you wonder? I will tell you the mystery of the woman [the Harlot System] and of the Beast [Antichrist] that carries her, which has the seven heads [seven previous Beast Empires: Egypt, Assyria, Babylon, Medo-Persia, Greece, Rome, and Hitler's 3rd Reich] and the ten horns [which make up Antichrist's 10-Nation Confederation of the 8th Beast Empire]. 8 The Beast [Antichrist] that you saw was [a leader of the one of the previous Beast Empires], and is not [because he is still yet to come in the future at the time of John's writing], and is about to come up out of the Abyss [the Bottomless Pit] and go to destruction [at the Battle of Armageddon at the 7th Bowel Judgment]. And those who dwell on the earth, whose name has not been written in the book of life from the foundation of the world, will wonder [be amazed] when they see the Beast [Antichrist], that he was [alive as a leader of one of the seven previous Beast Empires] and is not [in existence at the time of John's writing] and will come [again as the leader of the 8th Beast Empire]. 9 Here is the mind which has wisdom. The seven heads are seven mountains [the previous Beast Empires] on which the woman [Harlot Babylon] sits, 10 and they are seven kings [the leaders of Egypt, Assyria, Babylon, Medo-Persia, Greece, Rome, Hitler's 3rd Reich]; five [leaders] have fallen [Egypt, Assyria, Babylon, Medo-Persia, and Greece] one is [Rome, at the time of John's vision], the other has not yet come [Hitler's 3rd Reich]; and when he [Hitler] comes, he must remain a little while. 11 The Beast which was [a leader of one of the previous seven Beast Empires] and is not [because he is still yet to come in the future], is himself also an eighth [Antichrist, the leader of the final Beast Empire that rules the world] and is one of the seven, and he goes to destruction [when he is killed at the Battle of Armageddon on the 1,290th day past the Midpoint and then cast into the Lake of Fire]. 12 The ten horns [ten leaders] which you saw are ten kings who have not yet received a kingdom [because they are still yet in the future], but they receive authority as kings with the Beast [Antichrist] for one hour [seven years]. 13 These have one purpose, and they give their power and authority to the Beast [Antichrist]. 14 These will wage war against the Lamb [Jesus Christ], and the Lamb will overcome them [at the Battle of Armageddon], because He is Lord of lords and King of kings, and those who are with Him {are the} called and chosen and faithful." Revelation 17:7-14 (Square brackets and underline inserted by the author for clarity of context.)

Verse 11 is a Key

Antichrist, a leader of one of the seven previous Beast Empires, was not in existence when John wrote of him because he was yet to come in the future (verse 10b). Moreover, one of the seven leaders of the seven previous beast empires is himself the eighth (verse 11), that is, the leader of the 8th Beast Empire which is none other than Antichrist.

Antichrist is destroyed in the Battle of Armageddon (verse 11) as described in the 7th Bowl Judgment which is 1,290 days after he declares himself to be God Almighty and demands everyone to receive his Mark (Daniel 12:11) and worship him.

You Must Choose Between Seven Leaders

Scripture limits our choice to seven men as proven by the record of history coinciding with the prophecies of both Daniel and Revelation.

To explain this, I'll combine all four clues in concert one with the other. Accordingly, the 4th Clue directly connects him to his "previous" leadership as one of the seven Beast Empires.

Fourth Clue...His Origin

Revelation 17:11 confirms that Antichrist is one of the previous beast leaders who suffered a fatal headwound. All of the leaders of the seven beast empires are now dead. But Antichrist, being one of the previous seven, has been kept alive in the Abyss.

The Abyss and the Bottomless Pit are different names for the same location. It is a place where certain types of spirits come and go.

For some types of spirits, once they are cast into the Abyss, they cannot escape. Recall the event when Jesus met the man of Gadara by the tombs (Luke 8:26-39). He was possessed by a legion of demons. When they saw Jesus, they begged Him not to cast them into the Abyss.

Human spirits living in hell cannot leave. That much we know. The Abyss, however, is different. Select spirits residing in the Abyss do not have the same restraint as the spirits of people living in hell.

In the 5th Trumpet Judgment of Revelation, hideous inde-scribable creatures come out of the Abyss and torment all who have the Mark of the Beast for five months without ceasing. Their torment is so severe, people will seek death and not be able to die.

Then, at the beginning of the 1,000-Year Reign of Jesus, Satan is bound by a chain and locked in the Abyss until the 1,000 years are over.

In addition to Antichrist, Scripture indicates that one of Satan's chief fallen angels (Abaddon, known as the angel of the Abyss) comes out of the Abyss (Revelation 9:11).

Accordingly, Revelation clearly states that Antichrist comes up from the Abyss:

> The Beast that you saw was [one of the seven leaders of the Beast Empires], and is not [because he is still yet to come in the future], and is about to come up out of the Abyss [Bottomless Pit] and goes to destruction [when he is killed at the Battle of Armageddon]. Revelation 17:8a (Square brackets inserted by the author for clarity of context.)

Many Christians are conflicted on how to reconcile someone coming back to life and ruling the world. This is especially true considering the following verse of Scripture:

> And inasmuch as it is appointed for men to die once and after this comes judgment.
> Hebrews 9:27

The Apostle Paul succinctly says that those who die in Christ are immediately taken to Heaven to be with the Lord.

> We are of good courage, I say, and prefer rather to be absent from the body and to be at home with the Lord. II Corinthians 2:5-8

But what of those who are not in Christ? The unsaved are immediately cast into hell just as the "saved" are immediately taken to Heaven.

The emphasis of Hebrews 9:27 centers on the aspect of *judgment*. When a person dies, *judgment* is fixed from the standpoint of their destiny. Yet beyond such judgment, we are not fully informed by Scripture as to the strict limitations of imprisoned human spirits.

Based on these observations, it seems the Abyss (the Bottomless Pit) is an access point where certain condemned spirits reside, yet without the same limitations as those locked in hell.

As to anyone coming back from the dead and living out their remaining days of mortal life, Scripture provides several examples: Lazarus came back from the dead to live out the rest of his natural life (John 11:1-44); Dorcas was resurrected from the dead when Peter prayed for her and she lived out her

116

natural life (Acts 9:40); Jairus' daughter was brought back from the dead and lived out her natural life (Mark 5:40-43); the man raised from the coffin by Jesus during the funeral process at Nain lived out his natural life (Luke 7:11-17); at the time of Christ's death on the cross, certain graves were opened and the Saints walked the streets of Jerusalem (Matthew 27:50-54). Finally, others in the Bible, were resurrected from the dead and lived out their mortal years only to die again.

As to Antichrist, he died as an eternally condemned man during his leadership of a previous Beast Empire. Unique only to him, he was kept from going to hell or he could not return from there according to prophecy. In this regard, he was taken into the Abyss where, as stated before, certain spirits come and go.

In any case, Scripture does not indicate the mechanics of how Antichrist has come up from the Abyss, or how his physical body has been restored and preserved. The declaration of this event is evident in Scripture, but the explanation of *how* is not given.

Suffice it to say he is already judged and is eternally damned. In this sense, he meets the requirement of Hebrews 9:27 wherein he is judged and cannot be saved. But note: in the passage of Hebrews, there is no specific qualifier that defines the strict limits of *after-death judgment*, especially as it applies to Antichrist coming up from the Abyss.

Considering All Four Prophecies

By using the four prophetic clues found in Scripture his identity is absolutely certain.

1. He is Magogic in lineage.

2. He died of a previous headwound.

3. He was a leader one of the previous Beast Empires.

4. He comes up from the Abyss.

From here, consider the lineage of the Seven Beast Empires stemming from the three sons of Noah. Specifically, we are looking for the lineages pertaining to the Magogic line:

1. Egypt comes from **Ham.**

2. Assyria comes from **Shem.**

3. Babylon comes from either **Ham or Shem.**

The first three Beast Empires are immediately eliminated because none of them are from the lineage of Magog. The next four, however, are from Magog:

4. Medo-Persia comes from **Magog.**

5. Greece comes from **Magog.**

6. Rome comes from **Magog**.

7. Nazi Germany comes from **Magog**.

Of the last four empires, we examine the manner in which each of the leaders died:

1. Medo-Persia was Darius. He was killed by sword through the torso during battle.

2. Greece was Alexander the Great. He died from Malaria.

3. Rome was Nero: He committed suicide by a knife wound to his throat.

4. Nazi Germany was Hitler: He committed suicide by gunshot to the head.

Hitler is Antichrist!

Only Hitler fits three of the four "tangible" requirements listed in prophecy by the Bible. The fourth, which is spiritual, his coming up from the Abyss, is self-evident by the credibility of prophecy.

1. He comes from the Magogic lineage.

2. He was a leader of the 7th Beast Empire.

3. He died of a fatal headwound.

4. He has already come up from the Abyss.

The Abyss

His coming up from the Abyss was a hidden event concealed from humanity. Nonetheless, based on the veracity of God's Word and the time in which we live, he is already a prolific leader on planet earth in some obscure position of government. His identity, however, is divinely hidden and cannot be recognized until God chooses the specific time.

Hitler and Satan

The other six leaders of the Beast Empires were polytheists. That is, they worshipped multiple gods. Only Hitler was obsessed with Satan and claimed that if he served him, Satan promised him a 1,000-year reign.

Of no surprise, the entire leadership of Nazi Germany was deeply consumed in the occult.

Will He Look Differently?

When Hitler assumes his role as Antichrist in the 8th Beast Empire, his face will be easily recognized as Hitler—the 3rd most familiar face on earth. He will not be in the body of another; he will be exactly who he was during the leadership of his Nazi 3rd Reich.

> I saw that one of the heads of the beast seemed wounded beyond recovery—but the fatal wound was healed! The whole world marveled at this miracle and gave allegiance to the beast. Revelation 13:3 TLB

Hitler's identity is likely protected by the Lord until he is revealed according to the purposes of God. After all, killing him would be morally justified since he is destined to murder ¼ of mankind. But, Antichrist must die exactly according to prophecy at the time of the 7th Bowl Judgment. Consequently, anyone standing next to him, or for that matter, having frequent contact with him, would not recognize him for who he actually is.

The time will come, however, when the veil is lifted and Hitler is fully revealed. Until he comes into his role at the opening of the 1st Seal of Revelation, he must remain hidden and kept in obscurity.

In this Critical Truth #5, the 4th dimension of the supernatural is now interfacing with our generation. The works of darkness we are now witnessing have never occurred before. This sobering reality puts us on line with the spiritual dimension. We are compelled, therefore, to acknowledge the spiritual powers in conflict, one with the other. Gone are the days of cozy uncontested Christian freedoms. A spiritual war rages in the unseen for which we must prepare by the power of the Holy Spirit in order to stand.

CHAPTER 6
CRITICAL TRUTH #6

Who Will Be Taken?

In this Critical Truth, many will be surprised that our walk with Jesus Christ requires a stricter partnership with Him than some suppose. Accordingly, the apathetic, complacent, lethargic, and indifferent Christian is in for a great shock.

> "Not everyone who says to Me, 'Lord, Lord,' will enter the kingdom of heaven, but he who does the will of My Father who is in heaven will enter. 22 "Many will say to Me on that day, 'Lord, Lord, did we not prophesy in Your name, and in Your name cast out demons, and in Your name perform many miracles?' 23 "And then I will declare to them, 'I never knew you; depart from me, you who practice lawlessness.'" Matthew 7:21-23

This may disturb some who are predisposed to one view of Scripture. You are therefore encouraged to let the Bible speak for itself in the very words and teachings of Jesus Christ.

Jesus Explains Key Event of This Generation

On April 7, 32 AD, Jesus sat privately with His disciples atop the Mount of Olives just outside of the City of Jerusalem. On their way to the Mount, they walked past the temple and His disciples commented on the magnificence of the temple buildings. Jesus immediately replied that a time would come when not one stone will be left on top of another.

As they sat overlooking the city, His disciples asked Him three questions wrapped into one:

> As He was sitting on the Mount of Olives, the disciples came to Him privately, saying, "Tell us, when will these things happen, and what {will be} the sign of Your coming, and of the end of the age?" Matthew 24:3

1. Tell us when these things will happen **[the destruction of the temple]**,

2. and what will be the sign of Your coming **[when You return]**,

3. and **[what are the signs]** of the end of the age? Matthew 24:3b

Jesus proceeds to answer their questions starting from Matthew 24:4 and finishes His explanation with the last verse of Matthew 25. Notably, the narration He gives does not use the same verbiage in the Book of Revelation because Revelation would not be written for another 64 years. Therefore, Jesus's uses different syntax in His narration when describing the same events of Revelation.

First, The Temple

In 70 A.D., Titus' army invaded Jerusalem and slaughtered every Jewish man, woman, infant, child, and pregnant woman they could find. In the course of the melee, the temple was destroyed exactly as Jesus said. Those who survived, fled Jerusalem and the land of Israel. They and their generations remained scattered among the nations without a country until Friday, May 14, 1948—1,878 years later. Thus, Jesus' words on Sunday and Monday of April 6 and 7, 32 A.D. were precisely fulfilled exactly as He said:

When He approached Jerusalem **[on Sunday, April 6, 32 A.D.]**, He saw the city and wept over it, 42 saying, "If you had known in this day, even you, the things which make for peace! But now they have been hidden from your eyes. 43 For the days will come upon you when your enemies will throw up a barricade against you, and surround you and hem you in on every side, 44 and they will level you to the ground and your children within you, and they will not leave in you one stone upon another, because you did not recognize the time of your visitation." Luke 19:41-44 (Square brackets inserted by the author for clarity of context.)

As Jesus continued with His description, the next thing He explained was the subject of His coming and the Rapture of the church which extends to Matthew 25 where He tells the parable of the Ten Virgins. This is a sober warning to all Christians, not to the world, but to those who claim to be in Christ. In this parable, He explains an alarming truth as it relates to a person's commitment to Jesus.

The Ten Virgins

Then the kingdom of heaven will be comparable to ten virgins, who took their lamps and went out to meet the bridegroom. 2 Five of them were foolish, and five were prudent. 3 For when the foolish took their lamps, they took no oil with them, 4 but the prudent took oil in flasks along with their lamps. 5 Now while the bridegroom was delaying, they all got drowsy and {began} to sleep. 6 But at midnight there was a shout, "Behold, the bridegroom! Come out to meet {him.}" 7 Then all those virgins rose and trimmed their lamps. 8 The foolish said to the prudent, "Give us some of your oil, for our lamps are going out." 9 But the prudent answered, "No, there will not be enough for us and you {too;} go instead to the dealers and buy {some} for yourselves." 10 And while they were going away to make the purchase, the bridegroom came, and those who were ready went in with him to the wedding feast; and the door was shut. 11 Later the other virgins also came, saying, "Lord, lord, open up for us." 12 But he answered, "Truly I say to you, I do not know you." 13 Be on the alert then, for you do not know the day nor the hour. Matthew 25:1-13

Separate the Picture-Pieces of the Parable

Let's separate the picture-pieces and discover their meanings. Notably, all ten persons are designated as "virgins". In the spiritual sense, this means they are innocent—their sins are forgiven and their names are written in the Lamb's Book of Life.

Their innocence is based on the finished work of Jesus whose effervescent blood remains as a continual cleansing effect against their sins.

The Virgins are NOT perfect, but innocent. Perfection is given to them on the day of the Rapture. Paul makes this distinction quite clear when he addressed the Corinthian church:

Behold, I tell you a mystery; we will not all sleep, but we will all be changed, 52 in a moment, in the twinkling of an eye, at the last trumpet; for the trumpet will sound, and the dead will be raised imperishable, and we will be changed. 53 For this perishable must put on the imperishable, and this mortal must put on immortality. I Corinthians 15:51-53

Next, the lamp represents their current state of life. Each of them have the Holy Spirit living within them (as represented by the oil), but there are differences between the Five Wise Virgins and the Five Foolish Virgins. The Five Wise Virgins are walking carefully in the fellowship of the Lord; the Five Foolish Virgins are playing in the world.

The foolish ones are shallow, indifferent, and living apart from the fellowship with the Holy Spirit. They might be in church on Sunday and display agreeable behavior in the company of their Christian peers, but inwardly they love the world more than the Kingdom of God. Still, they would not deny Jesus or the teachings of His righteousness.

As previously stated, the oil in their lamps represent the Holy Spirit. The brightness of the lamp's flame depicts the degree of fellowship they have with the Lord. The brighter the flame, the greater the fellowship. Conversely, a dimmer flame proves the degree of their compromised walk with the Lord.

A Picture of the Jewish Wedding

The parable of the Ten Virgins illustrates the culture of the Jewish wedding feast. Let me explain this part of the parable because without understanding it, the parable loses its impact.

In the Jewish culture, when a man and woman become engaged, the union is as strong as if the wedding had already taken place. Once she accepts his proposal, he goes and prepares a place for their new life. This is what Jesus referred to in John 14:13 when He said He goes to prepare a place for us and then He will return.

The bride, however, does not know the exact day or hour the groom will come for her. After all, buying land, building a house, acquiring livestock, or planting fields, even harvesting the crop, all require time. But once the groom determines everything is ready, he tells his friends that the time has come.

Runners (friends of the groom) advance before him in joyful celebration of his coming for the bride. This is the same as the prophets today telling the world that Jesus is coming.

This announcement quickly reaches the bride who makes herself "ready". The lamp in her window must burn brightly at all times. If she is derelict or indifferent, she might be unprepared when the groom comes for her.

When suddenly her groom arrives, he takes her to their new place. There, by invitation only, they celebrate a wedding feast comprised of family and friends.

In the parable of the Ten Virgins, we find ALL ten virgins are slumbering. This denotes the idea that in our generation very few expect Him in the prophetic season of His arrival.

In the parable, the word is given that the groom is on the way. This, as previously stated, is the unified prophetic voices of God's people today.

Suddenly, all Ten Virgins awake. This is the moment of reality—the time of certainty—the very moment of the 6th Seal when Jesus comes back.

All Ten Virgins awake and quickly trim their wicks so that the flame burns full and brightly. This is when the Five Foolish Virgins realize their demise. They appeal to the Five Wise Virgins to give them some of their oil. By comparison, the Five Wise Virgins have "extra" oil in their lamps. The foolish ones are running out of oil, and their flames are struggling to stay lit.

Reality strikes the heart and the Five Wise Virgins say:

"No, there will not be enough for us and you too; go instead to the dealers and buy some for yourselves."

Even though the Ten Virgins were grouped together as one, and even though they collectively enjoyed common "relationship" in the Lord, the Five Foolish Virgins lived a lifestyle "absent of fellowship". They only had relationship with Jesus, not fellowship.

They were not committed to Him or His righteousness. Perhaps they were carousing through the night on Friday and Saturday in drunken revelry but coming to church on Sunday morning from time to time.

Perhaps if they had more time, they might have spiritually matured and overcome their foolishness. But time is not afforded them for such changes. Time is interrupted by the sudden appearance of the Groom.

As the parable continues, the Five Foolish Virgins have no options. They have no time to change their lifestyle which is proven by the course of time.

"Character" is not forged in a moment—it is cultivated as a lifestyle. Consequently, even though the Five Foolish Virgins regret their unacceptable and compromised lifestyle, they do not have enough time to credibly prove a life of commitment.

At last the groom comes. The Five Wise Virgins enter the wedding feast with the groom (Jesus) and the door is shut. The door being shut denotes the moment of the Rapture. The Five Foolish Virgins pound at the door begging to be let in, but it is too late. Jesus answers the door, and says, "Truly I say to you, I do not know you."

The Word "Know"

There are key words in the Greek that render a better understanding of what Jesus said than the English language provides pertaining to the word, "know".

Ginosko, is a word frequently used in Scripture. It means, in a general sense, to have close relationship or to be experientially intimate. Hence, "You shall "ginosko" the truth and the truth shall make you free."

Knowing the truth is not academic. Knowing the truth is experiential and living the principles of the truth is a lifestyle. *Ginosko* is the same word often used for intimacy between a husband and a wife.

Jesus does not use *Ginosko* in the parable when he says, "Truly I say to you, I do not "know" you." Instead, He uses the word *eido*.

Eido signifies that He sees them, He recognizes their presence, but He does not acknowledge them. They lived a life of "eido", not "ginosko", with the Lord. They acknowledged Him, but they never lived a life of intimate fellowship with Him.

The Door is Shut

The closed door means the Rapture of the Saints has taken place and the Five Foolish Virgins are left behind. This parable destroys the idea that a person only needs to say they are a Christian and all is well.

The consequential moment of the Rapture is unlike any time in the interplay between God and man. This parable sends a sober warning that the Rapture event is a discriminating moment, an interruption in the timeline of this generation when God suddenly arrives for those expecting Him who are also living for Him.

Gone are the days of our forefathers who had the privilege of living into their 90's and enjoying a full timeline to achieve intimacy with the Lord. Today, unlike the generations before us, we are an interrupted generation. As you are when He comes, your lifestyle determines whether you are Raptured or left behind. This is why Jesus said to be ready because He comes at an hour no one knows.

What About Those Left Behind?

It must be acknowledged that the Five Foolish Virgins had the Holy Spirit living within them. And while God's Spirit constantly besought their fellowship for a deeper walk in Christ, they did not choose to serve Him. Nonetheless, their names are written in the Lamb's Book of Life and it must be acknowledged that they have salvation.

Regrettably, they now undergo an intense refinement. Having the shocking reality of being left behind, they quickly sober to the moment. By default, they end up as martyrs for the Lord.

The Foolish Virgin types are those that comprise many of "post-Rapture martyrs". They will enter the 1,000 Year Reign of Jesus on earth with a natural physical body—not a glorified perfect body as the Five Wise Virgins. Consequently, they do not get their glorified body until after the White Throne Judgment.

> Then I saw thrones, and they sat on them, and judgment was given to them [at the Sheep and Goat Judgment]. And I {saw} the souls of those who had been beheaded because of their testimony of Jesus and because of the Word of God, and those who had not worshiped the Beast or his image,

and had not received the mark on their forehead and on their hand; <u>and they came to
life</u> and reigned with Christ for a thousand
years. 5 The rest of the dead [those whose
names were not written in the Lamb's Book
of Life] did not come to life until the thousand
years were completed [where they are
judged and cast into the Lake of Fire]. This
is the first resurrection. Revelation 20:4-5 (Square
brackets and underline inserted by the author for clarity of
context.)

Specifically, this is the first resurrection "after" the rapture of the church.

Critical Truth #6

**It is imperative that you put away all besetting sins
and take your walk in Christ more seriously than ever before. Time is of the essence. This is the juncture in the an-
nals of humanity where the penalties are beyond anything
anyone comprehends.**

"Seeing we also are compassed about with
so great a cloud of witnesses, let us lay
aside every weight, and the sin which so
easily besets us, and let us run with pa-
tience the race that is set before us, looking
unto Jesus, the author and finisher of our
faith." Hebrews." 12:1-2 KJV

You MUST stay vitally connected to the fellowship of the Saints, specifically your church.

"On-line" church is NOT church, and it is NOT the fellowship with the Saints. Church requires face-to-face interaction, physical presence, and experiencing the spontaneous move of the Holy Spirit among the Saints. Therefore, find a solid church in tune with the times we live—one that is "power-filled" with the presence of His Holy Spirit and one that holds true to the very Word of God.

Conversely, avoid "seeker sensitive" or the Emergent Churches. They are as spiritually deep as a mud puddle. Their ambition is to keep their crowds religiously happy without confrontation or the urgency for change. These are the nesting places for the Five Foolish Virgins.

Avoid churches that refuse to accept the Word of God as absolute, without error, and unchangeable. These are those which Paul described by the Holy Spirit's warnings:

> For a time is coming when people will no longer listen to sound and wholesome teaching. They will follow their own desires and will look for teachers who will tell them whatever their itching ears want to hear. II Timothy 4:3

> But realize this, that in the last days difficult times will come. 2 For men will be lovers of self, lovers of money, boastful, arrogant, revilers, disobedient to parents, ungrateful,

unholy, 3 unloving, irreconcilable, malicious gossips, without self-control, brutal, haters of good, 4 treacherous, reckless, conceited, lovers of pleasure rather than lovers of God, 5 holding to a form of godliness, although they have denied its power; avoid such men as these. II Timothy 3:1-5

In the Critical Truth #6 you must take a sober inventory of your life. Deliberately plan time with Jesus in prayer, the study of His Word, and stay in the consistent fellowship of like-minded Saints. In this critical hour, you must repent and purge your life of besetting sins, calling on the Lord to lead you into a deeper fellowship with Him in every aspect of life. He is there to help you in this!

CHAPTER 7
CRITICAL TRUTH #7

Keep Your Eyes on Israel

In this Critical Truth, you will learn why Israel is both the trigger and the key to the Endtime events that sets the Book of Revelation into motion. Unfortunately, Israel is rarely given serious consideration. As a result, the prophetic importance of Israel escapes the notice of many Christians altogether.

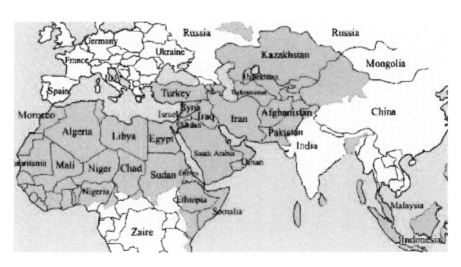

In Critical Truth #7, you will learn specifically what signs to look for that cluster around Israel, and the countdown to escape to your refuge—even to the very day.

When one thinks of "nations" and their impact, Israel's size is somewhat surprising. Few people realize it is the smallest nation in the world and can fit within the state of Texas 32 times! Given its size, therefore, how could such a tiny nation have such major global impact?

Aside from the fact that Israel is the Apple of God's Eye, His covenant nation, He will never abandon her. Israel is also the birthplace of three passionate major world religions that are in conflict one with the other: Judaism, Christianity, and Islam. Over the past millenniums, Israel has been the intersection of continual conflicts. Even today it is a cauldron of unrest and war. Oddly enough it is also the seat of salvation for mankind because through Israel came Jesus Christ.

As shown on the map where Israel is but a tiny red shape of a nation, consider the overwhelming landmass of the Islamic nations that surround her which are colored in green.

To say the least, this is a serious problem for Israel. Israel is nestled in the region of frequent attacks because of anti-Israel sentiments promoted by the Islamic nations, particularly, Iran.

Of all the Islamic nations, Iran is Israel's nemesis that never rests. Even in the eyes of other Islamic nations, Iran is considered a dangerous rogue nation soon to be in possession of nuclear weapons.

The sanctity of life means nothing to Iran's godless leaders. Added to this, Iran is also the harbor of international terrorism. Of no surprise, Iran's religious and political leaders are suffused with hatred against Israel and want her wiped off the earth.

Iran's problem, however, is two-fold in nature: First and foremost, it is God Almighty. Israel is God's favored nation—the apple of His eye. And even though Islam and Judaism both claim Abraham as their covenant father, the god of Islam is not the God of Abraham, Isaac, and Jacob. Proponents of Islam, such as Barack Obama, would have people believe that Islam and Christianity serve the same God. Nothing could be further from the truth. Neither Christianity or Islam would agree with that statement.

Second, America currently favors Israel. But a time will come, such as we saw with US President, Barak Obama, that America will lessen the support of Israel. Eventually, Israel's covering will be removed as it relates to America's slowly evolving policy toward godlessness.

We are again peaking toward that sentiment within America right now. America's move toward humanism is taking us further and further from the oracles of God's righteousness and back to the proverbial Tower of Babel. Consequently, America is progressively drifting away from Israel.

Iran and America

Iran has broken every treaty made with the Western nations, and more specifically, America. In the doctrines of Islam, lying is acceptable if it is a tool to reach a positive conclusion.

Because it was politically expedient, former US President, Barak Hussain Obama, claimed to be a Christian when he ran for the office of the US President. At the same time, in juxtapose to his Christian veneer, he was a fervent champion of the Islamic faith. The two faiths are contrary, one against the other at the core of their very teachings. For instance, according to the Quran in the book of Surah 9:29, it says, *"Fight*

139

those who don't believe in Allah or in the Last Day, and don't forbid the things that Allah and His Apostle have forbidden; and who don't have Islam, the religion of truth, as their religion; from among the Jews and Christians—until they pay the fine for being non-Muslims, and have been humiliated."

Obama very tactfully avoided celebrating the National Day of Prayer by claiming it did not represent all faiths. But during that same year he hosted a dinner at the White House in celebration of Ramadan—a sacred time of fasting under the Islamic beliefs where Muslims eat one meal a day. During Ramadan, he removed all jewelry, including his wedding ring.

The only Scriptures Obama quoted in public (and routinely misapplied their context) were those which the Islamic clerics deemed uncontaminated by non-Islamic people.

He stands in history as the only US President that danced between his Christian façade and his personal practices of Islam. This would include his visits to the Islamic Mosque in Baltimore on February 2, 2016 in order to pray.

As the picture shows, he was the first and only US President that bowed to an Islamic king—the King of Saudi Arabia. Among Obama's self-serving opinions representing America, he declared to the world that America was no longer a Christian nation—his view, not the opinion of the American people.

It was Obama that vigorously promoted an international campaign mandating that all nations accept the LGBTQ agenda into their societies. Those who refused would be disqualified from receiving US financial aid.

He also persuaded the Prime Minster of Great Britain to join him in this abominable promotion. Accordingly, Great Britain denied financial aid to the nations of their commonwealth unless they accepted the LGBTQ agenda.

When presented with the option by Great Britain, Ghana President, Atta Mills, told the British Prime Minister to keep his money as they would rather be pleasing to the Lord than to Great Britain:

"Mr. Atta Mills… told the BBC, the [Ghana] government would not compromise its morals for money. If that aid is going to be tied to things that will destroy the moral fibre of society, do you really want that?" he told the BBC's Focus on Africa programme.[23]

Obama—The American Forerunner Against Israel

Obama's personal disdain for Israel was effectively stifled from the public exposure by his political strategies. In contrast, he openly stood with his Islamic brother's by supplying them with financial aid, advanced military grade weapons, and political endorsements. To counterbalance his zealous appearance for Islam, he masked his true feeling against Israel by allocating her the customary US financial aid. Of course, this was merely a front. Money of itself does little for

---

[23] Some 41 nations of the British Commonwealth have laws banning homosexual practices. https://www.bbc.com/news/world-africa-15558769

protection, especially as he empowered her enemies at the same time.

To demonstrate this point, consider the following article from an interview on the radio: *Israel National Radio's* Weekend Edition with host, Tamar Yonah.

"(IsraelNIN.com) An unnamed former highly-placed U.S. intelligence official has broken silence and says that America may soon be abandoning Israel [under Obama] in favor of the Arabs. "This is just the beginning," he said, "Israel could be about to lose the support of the United States."

"The source made these remarks in an exclusive interview with Douglas J. Hagmann,[24] the director of the Northeast Intelligence Network (NIN), which is comprised of veteran licensed professional investigators, analysts, military affairs specialists, and researchers. The group has combined their resources to provide accurate and well-sourced information via their website."

Will Morally Destitute America Abandon Israel?

"When questioned about the possible abandonment of Israel by America, Hagmann told Yonah, "The Obama administration is no friend to Israel, is no friend to the Jews in America, and is no friend to democracy or freedom in America…just by his very appointments, we can see him filling positions of power with people who are anti-Semitic, who want

---

[24] Hagmann appeared on *Israel National Radio's* Weekend Edition with host Tamar Yonah.

to see Israel essentially dissolved as a nation, if not by diplomacy, then certainly by war."

"In his report, the unnamed intelligence source told Hagmann, "I have every reason to believe, based on what I've seen at my level of [security] clearance especially over the last several years, that Israel will soon be completely on their own…or worse." He explained this would happen "when our administration provides more support to Arab countries [with] financial and military aid, undercutting Israel's defense efforts all while pushing Israel to succumb to the pressure of unreasonable demands designed to end with their political annihilation as a nation."

"Hagmann told Yonah that this official broke silence because he had already retired from his highly placed position, and because of his knowledge of the NIN's (Northeast Intelligence Network) position as pro-Israel, and the way it valued the relationship between Israel and America. Another reason, he said, was his own perception of the Biblical aspect of this scenario developing."

"The intelligence officer explained that the turnover of American policy towards Israel could occur through a manner that he dubbed "malicious intelligence," which Hagmann defined as information that is taken from its raw form. It then is morphed into something else to promote different interests, "where intelligence and politics meet and often collide," he said. A method "that has been molded and massaged to advance the agendas of a select few," he elaborated.

"In the case of the relationship between America and Israel, he noted, malicious intelligence is being used to turn over the U.S. to a more anti-Israel policy and forge ahead with a more pro-PA or pro-Islamist one.

"Hagmann told Yonah in the radio interview, "A perfect example of this is when there was a shooting in Seattle a couple of years ago at a Jewish center. The police were ordered by the city officials and by the Federal Government, basically, to not protect the synagogues and other Jewish centers in Seattle, but to have protection details [instead] at the mosques in Seattle."

"U.S. administrations have apparently been following a policy of abandoning Israel for several years, according to Hagmann's report. His interview with the intelligence official cited "the 2005 surrender of Gush Katif to the Palestinian Authority as one essential example of the slow dismantlement of Israel as a viable nation. Despite essential intelligence outlining in every possible manner imaginable that this would be a disastrous move leading to the events we are seeing today [rocket and missile fire on Israel], it was done anyway," he stated.

"In the report that Hagmann posted he cited one of his sources explaining, "Now you can see where intelligence and politics meet and often collide... "The Obama administration is being purposely filled with people who are truly anti-Israel, either because of their own financial interests or a larger globalist agenda that does not include Israel, or for that matter, the United States as a sovereign nation.

"Whatever the reason, the anti-Israel, pro-Islamist policy makers will be appointed or have already infiltrated nearly all levels of the U.S. government. These are the people who place anti-Semitic references in school textbooks, promote revisionist history regarding Islam, 9/11, and are the same people who allow or even promote the Islamic agendas in all aspects of Western society, especially the restrictions on speech against Islam.

"With regard to the latter, note that the United Nations is quite involved in forcing the restriction of "hate speech" and the implementation of global standards, some that have already been adapted by European nations," noted the source.

"Hagmann reports that "the Middle East will be the site of 'the coming war,' and Israel will be at its epicenter. If we survive as a nation, the U.S. will not be on the side of righteousness in this war, instead turning our back to—or our guns against—our only true friend in the Middle East—Israel," he said."

★★★

Obama, as a sinister forerunner toward the abandonment of Israel, shows how Satan is subtly manipulating America's covering over Israel through such ungodly leaders.

Few people realize the network of evil assigned to America for being Israel's greatest ally. Satan cannot allow this roadblock to continue in his quest to destroy Israel and gain control of the world. Consequently, he needs leaders like Obama and those under him in places of government influence.

The nation [Israel] is like a mighty lion; when it is sleeping no one dares wake it. Whoever blesses Israel will be blessed, and whoever curses Israel will be cursed." Numbers 24:9 (Good News Translation)

But There Are Penalties...

By Obama's very actions against Israel, America incurred spiritual penalties. Under Obama, America's prosperity sagged in nearly every sector of her national well-being. As he threw punches against Israel, the world saw him as a weak failing leader without strong resolve.

With God's blessing over America diminished because of Obama, America's military was substantially weakened and the economy faded. Jobless rates reached epic proportions; socialism launched in greater fervor as a new government alternative; riots looting and unrest reached an all-time high, and racism resurged in massive proportions comparable to the days of Martin Luther King.

His failed "Obamacare" was eaten through with manipulations, misrepresentations, inconsistencies, and botched infrastructure. This drove medical costs to near unaffordable levels and placed more tax burdens on the American populace.

Under Obama's failed domestic policies, he alone added 74% more national debt, nearly 47% higher than his predecessor and 362% higher than Ronald Regan.[25]

In nearly every sector of American life, especially in middle-class America, Obama left massive deficit, controversy, and confusion. Until his successor, Joseph Biden, Obama ranked as America's worst president.

Obama was a spiritually dark trendsetter, an anomaly among the ranks of US Presidents—the first of his kind that worked against Israel by shifting the balance through supporting her enemies, specifically the Islamic nations. While he was giving Israel her annual customary US Aid, he was tossing even more dollars to her nemesis.

Unlike other US Presidents, he duped the American public with suave rhetoric and then radically changed to his real posture once he attained office.

He stands alone as the first President of the United States who, by his own words, is faithful to Islam and claimed the morning sing-song call to prayer from mosques around the world as the most melodious sound ever. He recited it in perfect Arabic:

God is the greatest (*Allahu akbar*); (said four times).

I testify that there is no God but Allah (*Ashhadu anna la ila ill Allah*); (said two times).

---

[25]https://www.thebalance.com/us-debt-by-president-by-dollar-and-percent-3306296

I testify that Mohammed is God's Prophet (*Ashhadu anna Muhammadan rasul Allah*); (said two times).

Come to prayer (*Hayya alas salah*); (said two times).

Come to security/salvation (*Hayya alal falah);* (said two times).

God is the greatest (*Allahu akbar);* (said two times).

There is no God but Allah (*La ilah ill Allah);* (said once).

No person that claims to be a genuine disciple of Jesus Christ could ever agree to any prayer sanctioning Mohammed and Allah, both of which are incompatible with the teachings of Jesus Christ. Yet, Obama did. Multiple times during his presidency he unwittingly revealed his love for Islam and his criticism of Christianity.

Is it any wonder he was the only President to flood America with Muslims from around the world and grant them citizenship by the airplane loads without any prior screening or documentation?[26]

He seeded various government offices in America with Islamic appointees in order to achieve changes in the political and religious climate of America. We now have officials

---

[26] "A total of 38,901 Muslim refugees entered the U.S. in fiscal year 2016, making up almost half (46%) of the nearly 85,000 refugees who legally entered the country in that period, according to a Pew Research Center analysis of data from the State Department's Refugee Processing Center. That means the U.S. has admitted the highest number of Muslim refugees of any year since data on self-reported religious affiliations first became publicly available in 2002."
https://www.pewresearch.org/fact-tank/2016/10/05/u-s-admits-record-number-of-muslim-refugees-in-2016/"

swearing their oath of office, not on the traditional Christian Bible, but on the Islamic Quran.

In accordance with Obama's Islamic tenets, he promoted and enabled Iran as much as he could without being excessively obvious. Consequently, even though Iran hates America, she found an ally with US President Obama.

As mentioned before, Iran, unlike other Islamic nations by comparison, is extreme, unstable, religiously irrational, and dominantly led by dark-spirited clerics that think nothing of destroying Israel and the US, if it were possible for them to do so.

How It All Comes Together

Iran proclaimed to the world that her nuclear powerplants are nothing more than, well, electrical power. However, since the time the U.S. withdrew from the nuclear pact because of Russian non-compliance, Iran has steadily progressed in her efforts of enriching uranium—the material needed for making nuclear warheads. In July 2019 for example, she began enriching uranium up to 5 percent; then to 20 percent in January 2021; and up to 60 percent in April 2021. Today, Iran is now on the precipice of producing weapons-grade nuclear material—heavy plutonium-239.

Heavy plutonium-239 is a substance, that by international agreement, cannot be sold. Consequently, Iran must produce her own plutonium-239 through the by-product of her nuclear power plants. Israel knows this; the world knows this; and Iran is denying it.[27]

The former President of Israel, Benjamin Netanyahu, addressed the United Nation in an appeal to employ economic restraints against Iran if she continued amassing the nuclear grade material in order to make a nuclear warhead.

Defiantly, however, Russia has been assisting Iran in that effort. Netanyahu was correct when he said Iran would destabilize the entire Middle East including the world if it came into possession of such weapons. His plea was ignored.

A Perfect Storm is Coming

Iran is backed by North Korea, Russia, and China, which are assisting Iran with the technology to get their nuclear systems up and moving.

Meanwhile, Israel is carefully monitoring Iran's developments and preparing for the worst. She will not and cannot afford to ignore the looming threat of an insane nation led by

---

[27] In practical terms, there are two different kinds of plutonium to be considered: reactor-grade and weapons-grade. The first is recovered as a by-product of typical used fuel from a nuclear reactor, after the fuel has been irradiated ('burned') for about three years. The second is made specially for the military purpose, and is recovered from uranium fuel that has been irradiated for only 2-3 months in a plutonium production reactor. The two kinds differ in their isotopic composition but must both be regarded as a potential proliferation risk, and managed accordingly. Plutonium, both that which is routinely made in power reactors and that which comes from dismantled nuclear weapons, is a valuable energy source when integrated into the nuclear fuel cycle. In a conventional nuclear reactor, one kilogram of Pu-239 can produce sufficient heat to generate nearly 8 million kilowatt-hours of electricity.

extreme radical Islamic leaders that religiously justify the genocide of the Jews.

Even though the bond between Israel and America is weakening, America still remains as Israel's strongest ally today. It was US President Truman whom the Lord used to declare Israel as a sovereign nation in 1948, and it was US President Trump that moved the US Embassy to Jerusalem, thus declaring, along with Israel, that Jerusalem is the capital of Israel. This infuriated the Islamic nations who claim Jerusalem as the seat of *their* religious faith—Islam.

The final component of the perfect storm will occur when America pulls away from Israel, which, current to this writing, she is doing in graduated degrees under the very weak leadership of President Biden—Obama's former Vice President. Evidently the apple did not fall far from the tree as both men are incredibly immoral leaders who are froth with lies, deceit, and self-rewarding policies.

As America backs further away from Israel because of American anti-Israel officials like Obama, or a mentally incapable leader like Biden, or because America is economically or militarily crippled by poor leadership, Israel will eventually stand alone. When that occurs, the potential war with Iran will reach DEFCON 1.

A Prediction of Reasonable Certainty

With America's shield over Israel diminished, and Iran in possession of nuclear weapons, Israel will fundamentally be without covering. I predict (not as in prophecy) that she will attack Iran's nuclear powerplants as well as Iran's nuclear missile sites. When she does, an international multi-nation alliance (largely from the Islamic nations) will come together under the bond of Islam and war will commence.

When war erupts, the Gulf of Hormouz will close soon thereafter. This is the shipping route that delivers crude oil to the world from the OPEC nations and Russia. Worldwide energy prices will spike—an irritation by which the world will blame Israel for driving up the costs of nearly everything.

Looking at the map once more, the nations colored in gray are Islamic. Most of them will join forces with Iran in the counter attack against Israel if for nothing more than to get the gulf opened again.

When the collection of overwhelming military forces join together against Israel, it will be more than she can handle, and her annihilation will be imminent. In order to survive, prophecy indicates she will call out to the nations of the world for help. A strong nation will come to her aid, which, by all apparent factors, will be none other than Russia, along with two other nations joined to Russia that are with Russia's developing confederation. Israel will then be offered a 7-Year Peace Pact that forces Israel's enemies to stand down.[28]

When Israel signs the Peace Pact, the 1st Seal of Revelation opens. You then have 1,260 days before the Mark of the Beast is imposed upon all mankind under penalty of death.

---

[28] Russia is the "go-to" nation in the Middle East today with submarine bases in Lebanon and a treaty with Syria for Syria's protection. She is also a strong ally with Iran and has strong relationships with other Islamic nations.

Antichrist's Spiritual Endorsements

At the time of the 4th Seal, the False Prophet (Antichrist's cohort) will affirm Antichrist's claim that Antichrist is God. This will be announced by the global media systems. But to prove the False Prophet's spiritual authority to make such declaration, he performs a supernatural demonstration and calls down a sustained pillar of fire from heaven for all the world to see. He then orders everyone to receive the Mark of the Beast and commands them to make an image of Antichrist and worship it. The penalty of death is imposed upon all who refuse.

The 4th Seal, if you recall, releases the Pale Horse which is Death and Hades. The command to worship Antichrist marks the beginning of the Tribulation where eventually over 1,975,000,000 people are killed, or a number equal to ¼ of mankind. Accordingly, these specific factors are given in Scripture so that you can know what to watch for:

1. A great war with Israel.
2. 1st Seal of Revelation opens with the signing of the 7-Year Peace Pact.
3. The countdown of 1,260 days begins so that you can prepare.
4. After the last day of 1,260 days, the 4th Seal opens to begin the Tribulation Period.

Again, the only thing Jesus instructed was to flee into the wilderness. Martyrdom will commence in Jerusalem and rapidly spread throughout the world. All nations will align with Antichrist's new world government under the power of his 10-Nation Confederation.

Remember, your timeframe is based on the given number of 1,260 consecutive days starting from the 1st Seal to the 3rd Seal in order to prepare. It is doable. It can be accomplished, and many people will successfully avoid Antichrist with the help of God as their covering.

Do not fear. Rather, live by faith and let the Holy Spirit guide you in your preparations. For this reason, it is imperative that you have rich fellowship in the Holy Spirit in order to develop a sensitivity to His leading. More will be discussed pertaining to that Critical Truth in the coming chapter.

In Critical Truth #7, keep your eye on Israel. When this pivotal world war breaks out, and America removes her covering, Israel's destruction will seem absolute. This is the moment when Russia comes to her aid. It is the moment when the 7-Year Peace Pact, a covenant with death, is signed by Israel. Then, immediately after 1,260 days has elapsed, know and understand, that you have reached the middle of the 7-Year Peace Pact. This is the timeframe when Antichrist suddenly invades Jerusalem and kills two out of three Jews in the streets. From that moment forward, he moves into the newly built temple in Jerusalem, takes his seat, (likely on the mercy seat on the Ark of the Covenant) and declares himself as God Almighty.

CHAPTER 8
CRITICAL TRUTH #8
What You Should be Doing Now!

In this Critical Truth, all doubt will be erased as to what you should be doing right now in order to prepare for the impending events of the Middle East that are currently in motion where war is inevitable.

What you are about to read may seem unbelievable because we have no historic reference to draw from the wisdom or example of those before us. Nonetheless, God's Word cannot lie.

Preparing for the 1,260-day countdown almost seems surreal, like the script of a science fiction movie. This is the material that Hollywood uses for their box office hits.

What makes this so challenging is the contrast of life today as compared to what is coming. Currently, we live in somewhat peaceful times, unless, of course, you live in Israel under the constant threats and attacks from the Palestinian-Islamic people.

In the natural, the coming events seem preposterous—a quantum leap into the implausible. This same mindset prevailed in the people of Noah's day when he tried convincing them that the earth would flood until the mountains were covered. Noah was speaking concepts beyond the experience of his generation by describing an unimaginable disaster at a time when it had never yet even rained (Genesis 2:4-6).

Keep Your Eyes on Israel

Keep your eyes on Israel and the prophecies pertaining to her demise. These are your timepieces. With those facts in mind, we turn our awareness to the inevitable reality of the coming 1,260-Day Period that opens with the 1st Seal of Revelation.

You need to be watching for THE war with Israel where she faces overwhelming military forces inclined toward her total destruction upon which a rescue-nation comes forward and offers her a 7-Year Peace Pact. When Israel signs the offer, the opening of the 1st Seal begins and the countdown of 1,260 days starts.

In all of this, we can be assured of the Holy Spirit's leading and guiding for us. Above all, this is not the time to panic. Fear and faith cannot function together in the same space at the same time. Your confidence must be perfectly centered in Jesus and nothing else.

First and Foremost

Carefully examine your life *right now*. Give consideration to ANYTHING that deflects from your intensity in Jesus.

Eliminate anything that distracts you from His word and the fellowship of the Saints. Even now, if you take time to listen, the Holy Spirit is leading you.

"Consciously" set aside time for routine prayer and the study of God's Word. Failing to put purposeful arrangement toward these two things creates the opportunity for fear to seize your thoughts. This is the time where you need to calculate *everything* for the cause of survival. On that endeavor, there are several things to be soberly understood:

1. Do not expect every Christian you know to have the same insight, sensitivity, enthusiasm, or agreement pertaining to the crisis about to come upon the entire earth.

Noah preached about the coming flood for a full century. No one believed him. Today, a vast majority of Christians are fooled into a vacation-mindset that the Rapture will come before any persecution occurs. These will be the people that are languishing in a false security. They will be trapped in the horror of Antichrist's murderous campaign. Paul warned about this mind-set:

> While they are saying, "Peace and safety!" then destruction will come upon them suddenly like labor pains upon a woman with child, and they will not escape. I Thessalonians 5:3

Consequently, be wise in what you say to others and carefully consider those to whom you invest your precious time. Most people already live in *denial*, indifference, or total ignorance about the things soon to happen. Some are fooled by fallacious doctrine for which they will not listen to any truth that contradicts what they have always believed, or for that matter, "want" to believe.

Some merely want to argue about their view of Scripture. Some will mock and ridicule your position. Others will simply deny whatever you say. From such, politely dis-involve yourself. Time proves all things, and time is something you cannot waste.

2. Find a "Spirit-filled" church or a gathering of Spirit-filled Christians that are in step and pace with the Holy Spirit. Develop a likeminded trust concerning what you must be doing NOW. For many Christians, these truths are simply inconceivable at the level of their Scriptural maturity and knowledge.

It is the "Spirit-filled" Christians that operate in the gifts of the Holy Spirit, especially the gift of prophecy. This particular gift is invaluable as God speaks in real-time to His people.

In the early church, for instance, a well-known prophet named, Agabus, warned the Christians that a worldwide famine was coming (Acts 11:28). On the credibility of his prophecy, the churches immediately took action and made preparations to assist the poorer churches with contributions. They acted "immediately" on what was coming in the near future.

This is the time Christians need to give serious consideration to the voice of the prophets. For some, this causes an alarm because of the fear that false words might be given. But remember, you have the Holy Spirit within you that will confirm or deny the things uttered as to whether they are of the Lord, or coming from a different spirit (I Corinthians 14:29).

Communication is the basis of life; agreement is the power of unity. Where there is strife and unbelief everything of the darkness comes. It is essential, therefore, that the written Word of God, the Bible, is the agreed guideline for any criteria pertaining to spiritual matters.

3. Most important, you must stay in sensitive, consistent, and unbroken fellowship with the Lord. Stay in His Word! Pray with a consistent timeframe every day. Deliberately construct your time with the Lord by praying both in the Spirit (tongues) and in your natural language (I Corinthians 14:4; Jude 1:20; Eph 6:18).

The value of this cannot be quantified. It is the powerbase from which everything is established in the coming days. Accordingly, in pace with such times, He will draw you into deep intimacy with Him by His Holy Spirit. Make this your most important priority of all.

4. Constantly stay in the Word of God, very particularly in the New Testament, but do not ignore the Old Testament. Highlight the prophecies in both the Old Testament and New

159

Testament concerning the Endtimes, as well as the promises of the Lord pertaining to His faithfulness.

There are relevant truths and principles in both Testaments to be understood and applied in everyday living, especially in the Psalms that clearly intersect God's love, mercy, and compassion, in the throes of humanity.

It goes without saying, that a life pleasing to the Lord is naturally sensitive to the leading of the Holy Spirit. Therefore, all besetting sins must be put aside by the strength of God. A life of careful consideration in all that we do and say is a lifestyle such as the Five Wise Virgins modeled.

Those are the most important "spiritual" considerations. By staying deeply connected with the Lord, the unfathomable fear coming upon the whole world cannot have its desired effect in you. But let there be no doubt about it, the times will be challenging:

> Men's hearts [will be] failing them for fear, and for looking after those things which are coming on the earth: for the powers of heaven shall be shaken. Luke 21:26 (Square brackets inserted by the author for clarity of context.)

5. Your escape should be to the wilderness—a place completely off the grid that is undiscoverable, hidden, and untraccable. It is foolishness to think you can hide in plain view, or in subtle obscurity where anyone has access to you.

The beast images will be the monitoring and reporting system to Antichrist's disciples. These demonic audible voices, speaking through the Beast Images in each home, will direct Antichrist's disciples to anyone hiding in their cities, communities, or localities. As stated earlier, this is a time like nothing ever before in the history of humanity where the "spiritual" unveils itself in the realm of the "natural".

Your wilderness journey will likely be no more than about 1,100 days.[29] It does not have to be impossible or death-defying. Wise preparation makes the difference between difficult and practical.

Keep in mind that during the 1700's in America, the pilgrims moved westward through the wilderness. They faced the same challenges of wilderness survival, but with less material preparation and knowledge that you have today—and they admirably survived.

In the disclosures and information prophesied in the Scriptures, you are given the knowledge of exacting times and signs in order to prepare. Again, preparation makes for a very survivable reality with true peace.

---

[29] This number is not given in the Scriptures but is an "estimated" time- frame based upon other indicators between the Seal and Trumpet Judgments. It could well be less, but unlikely it will be more than that.

Then those who are in Judea must flee to the mountains. Those who are in Judea <u>must flee to the mountains</u>.17 Whoever is on the housetop must not go down to get the things out that are in his house. 18 Whoever is in the field must not turn back to get his cloak. 19 But woe to those who are pregnant and to those who are nursing babies in those days! 20 <u>But pray that your flight will not be in the winter, or on a Sabbath</u>. 21 For then there will be a great tribulation, such as has not occurred since the beginning of the world until now, nor ever will. 22 Unless those days had been cut short, no life would have been saved; but for the sake of the elect those days will be cut short. 23 Then if anyone says to you, 'Behold, here is the Christ,' or 'There *He is*,' do not believe *him*. 24 For false Christs and false prophets will arise and show great signs and wonders, so as to mislead, if possible, even the elect.
Matthew 24:16-24

Winter or Sabbath Flight

Why did Jesus focus on these two conditions in verse 20: the Sabbath and the winter? The answer, mostly, but not exclusively, applies to the Jews living in Jerusalem that will be basking in a false peace and false safety under Antichrist's 7-Year Peace Pact.

When Antichrist suddenly invades Jerusalem with his army between the 3rd and 4th Seals, there will be no time for anyone in Jerusalem to prepare. It will come unexpectedly and without warning. His invasion will be swift, calculated, and well executed. This is the moment he has planned from the onset of the Peace Pact—to move into the newly built temple in Jerusalem and declare himself as God Almighty.

The warning Jesus gives in Matthew 24:16-24 primarily focuses on the epicenter of Antichrist's sudden change from his White Horse Persona to his treacherous Pale Horse Persona when his global slaughter begins. The warning applies first to the Jews and then to the world. Unfortunately, exactly as Jesus said, the Jews will be totally deceived until Antichrist's invasion begins. By then, it is too late for them.

Obviously, as they slumber in false peace and security, they have no concern of escaping something where there is no threat.

In that regard, if Antichrist's invasion occurs during the winter, the weather will be a challenging issue for those suddenly thrust into the wilderness. If Antichrist attacks during the Sabbath, it will be a time when the city is essentially asleep. No businesses will be open to acquire last-second preparations such as food. But to you, the Christian, this time will not take you by surprise. You will know the exact day when Antichrist changes his persona. It is prophetically given and cannot be altered or changed

Timing for the Escape

By being well informed according to the prophecies, you will know when the 7-Year Peace Pact begins that ends the war with Israel. You will know when the 1,260-day countdown commences, and the day just before the Mark of the Beast is required. This invaluable foreknowledge is graciously provided by the Lord in His Word for all who take the time to read what He says.

By knowing in advance when the last day of the 1,260-Day Period arrives, you can reasonably prepare. For example: does the final day of the 1,260 days land in the middle of the winter; or the beginning of a cold rainy season; or the pleasantry of the summer months?

By knowing when the *first day* that the 7-Year Peace Pact begins, you can calculate 1,260 days later to determine what part of the season the final day arrives. This will help you determine when you need to be on location at your wilderness refuge. Obviously, you do not want to start your journey during the challenging seasons of weather. Therefore, with specific insight, you will know ahead of time when to be on location in order to make the required adjustments, improvements, and preparations such as constructing a root cellar, gathering of firewood, shelter improvements, and final adjustments for any unforeseen issues.

A Global Destruction

As previously stated, Antichrist's slaughter of mankind begins from the time of the 4th Seal and remains in full force until Jesus comes at the time of the 6th Seal. Antichrist's killing will be relentless, saturating, and vengeful against all who refuse to worship him.

Using the current population number of today, which is 7.9 billion people, Antichrist kills 1,975,000,000 people in a timespan "estimated" to be about 1,100 days in duration. By using that *estimated number of days* (and no one knows the exact length of time), over 75,000 people will die every single hour for the next 26,640 hours.

The timeframe could be substantially less than 1,100 days. If it is, it means the number of people killed per hour will increase. But again, it must be emphasized that no one knows precisely how long the Tribulation lasts.

Antichrist will not be able to kill everyone or there would be no Rapture of the living. The most vulnerable prey will be those caught unaware; those who believed in a "pre-tribulation" Rapture scenario and felt no need to prepare; or those who had no ability to flee for any number of reasons.

You, on the other hand, do not need to be a victim of his conquest. Therefore, knowledge and preparation is vital.

During Antichrist's campaign as people are captured, the choice will likely be given to each person to receive the Mark of the Beast and worship him, or die. Sadly, some, will defect and comply with Antichrist's demand by taking the Mark of the Beast. What they fail to realize is that they have only extended their life for 1,335 days "if" they survive the furious judgments of God's coming wrath that makes the earth a miserable habitation.

Characteristics of Your Refuge

Because there is no chance of survival within any community or the basement of a house, or a hideaway like Ann Frank, your refuge, as repetitively stated, MUST be off the grid—an area that affords you non-discovery. Accordingly, any location that requires public utilities or any other type of service is already a discoverable area.

Those living in the country on ranches, farms, or in remote areas are equally as unsafe, even if they can survive without dependence on public utilities such as fuel or electricity.

And for those who believe they can defend their land, no person can effectively amass enough weapons to withstand Antichrist's military systems.

"Off the grid" means going to a placed that is relatively undiscoverable, hidden, remote, separated from trails, rails, and roads. With this in mind, your refuge site can be anywhere in the world that meets this criteria.

Specific to your chosen location, you must take into consideration the skills, knowledge, and abilities needed to survive relative to the place of your choosing. Start developing those skills now!

For instance, there is no challenge for an Eskimo living in the cold tundra. He understands how to hunt for food through the ice and under the ice; he knows what kind of clothing is needed; and he understands how to construct a livable shelter. He is acclimated to his environment. But to someone living in Florida all their life, this would be an extreme contrast.

166

Therefore, give careful consideration regarding the area you choose based on your abilities, needs, physical tolerance, etc.

1. After much prayer, pick a place suitable to your abilities and analyze the surroundings. Remember, NO ONE should know your location. If there are trails leading into the "general area", then a high probability exists that it is already discoverable.

2. Idaho's INEEL has mapped every state in the union by satellite that shows all geothermic locations ranging from a coffee-cup-trickler, to a full-on commercial recreation site. If you find a location that provides year-round geothermic energy, it would be a major bonus.

3. Your location should have an adequate abundance of the flora and fauna (plants and animals). Eatable plants indigenous to your area should be studied in order to safely distinguish them from poisonous plants that are similar in appearance. Some plants can be eaten raw; others MUST be cooked.

Study various mushroom types that are safe and edible; study various herbal medicine plants and remedies. Also, consider the streams and rivers as good locations for indigenous types of wildlife. Where there is water, there is life. Learn the various types of animals suitable for consumption that you normally would not consider such as rabbit, beaver, game birds, wild-caught fish, etc.

4. Limit your community of people to a small number between 25 to 30 or less. The larger the community, the higher the probability of discovery, and the greater the impact on

your location for basic essential needs. If personal pets are considered, remember they require food. Domestic pets do not have natural survival instincts. They depend on you to provide them with food and shelter.

5. People with preexisting medical conditions need to carefully plan by collecting medicines and such for their specific needs. By God's grace, you should expect the Holy Spirit's help in healings and miracles.

6. Guns and ammo / bow and arrow / sling shots / traps and snares/ fishing poles: These are for acquiring food and safety against wild animals. The inexpensive .22 caliber is perhaps the best for this. Currently, such ammo is easily procured. Start buying now. A rifle is better than a pistol for accuracy sake.

A word of caution regarding the use of firearms: first, they are loud and attract attention. Second, any consideration for fighting against Antichrist is futile. Third, you must carry the necessary equipment for the cleaning and operation of the firearm. Rust is a factor for all ferrous metals such as knives, axes, saws, etc. Because firearms are precision-made instruments, they must be well maintained in a safe clean operating condition.

The bow and arrow is quiet, effective, but it also has maintenance requirements depending on the type of bow and the arrows. Extra supplies should be considered for all components of this type of tool including the draw string, arrows, and rail lube if you use a crossbow.

Fishing line, lures, hooks, and terminal tackle must be carefully considered. This is NOT sport fishing. It is food gathering. A stronger heavier line is better. Generally speaking, braided line is longer lasting than monofilament.

You need to develop skills with everything used to acquire food. Practice them NOW.

7. If the choosing of your place is initially decided upon by a topo map or satellite imagery, it is important that you physically go on location well in advance and explore the land. I suggest you do this at the earliest possible opportunity. This is a time-consuming and laborious effort.

Once you are on location, look for consistently running clean water systems; distances from various observation points and locations; distances to various food source areas like flowing rivers or valleys, etc.

Bring seeds for planting. If you decide it is a safe and sustainable location, plant your crops and let them go to seed.

Study the growing season and geography for the types of crops that grow in the specific soils and climate specific to the place you choose. Altitude places a major role in the growing season. Again, by all means, once you decide on a location, visit your site several times to carry in the necessary equipment before you make your final move. It is impractical to assume you can carry everything to your site in one trip.

When first exploring the area, avoid the use of devices that produce an electronic signature or registers traceable signals such as cell phones or GPS tracking instruments—anything that uses satellite signals. Also keep in mind that too many visits using the same pathway or route produces trackable signs upon the land. Therefore, when making multiple approaches, use different routings to and from, even if the route is only a few hundred yards apart.

8. No electronics! As previously stated, when you decide to scout your area, avoid the use of cellphones, satellite GPS systems—anything that leaves a traceable electronic print. Travel by map and compass. Develop that skill NOW. On the day you finally move to your refuge location, *before* you leave civilization, remove the batteries and power-down all electronic equipment—everything! Destroy them and leave them behind! This is especially true of portable satellite radios.

Cellphones have traceable stored data and can be "pinged" by technology to listen to conversations and enable tracing. Cellphones maintain satellite connection even when powered-down. Therefore, know the specific details of whatever electronic devise you own. Assume none of them are safe.

AM/FM and multiband radios are harmless as they pick *up* signals but do not transmit signals via satellite. Handheld two-way radios can be a problem if they over-transmit in a broad area from a high vantage point. Be sure to avoid two-way handheld radios that use satellite connections.

Conversely, multiband radios designed with variable power systems such as hand-crank, solar panel, and rechargeable batteries, are important *for monitoring world events and even weather reports.*

9. On the market today, one can obtain reasonably priced electric solar panels capable of recharging batteries as well as running small electric lighting. This type of apparatus can be quite resourceful, affordable, and easily purchased. Prepare now for such items.

10. Your refuge is to be kept a secret. Guard against any disclosure. Do not share any information about your refuge site, preparations, or even their potential location through cell phone, electronic public media systems, or by cryptic messages, etc. Remember, these instruments have traceable data systems and are currently monitored by the government. Snowden and the NSA proved how the government is monitoring all communication systems in America. Whatever you advance in knowledge via the Internet, cell phones, or anything via satellite communication devises is discoverable.

11. Your selection of people that come with you must be carefully considered, proven, and spiritually discerned. Gone are the days where people simply float in and out of Christian gatherings without commitment to Christ or one another.

In China, for example, admission to the underground churches is granted only if a person is first proven on the credibility of three people. When you allow unproven and uncommitted persons that claim to be Christians into your group, you risk the wellbeing of everyone.

Those whom you select in your trusted circles must be mindful of how important non-disclosure is to your plans and intentions. Teamwork is essential.

12. Even with the best of intentions, there are risks of defection and as a result, discovery. This is why you must be led by the Holy Spirit in all that you do.

Some people, for whatever reason, will fall into spiritual seduction and change their mind concerning their commitment to Jesus Christ. Therefore, a brother today can be the enemy tomorrow.

> **Brother will betray brother to death, and a father his child; and children will rise up against parents and have them put to death.**
> Mark 13:12

Accordingly, do not presume that your untested and unproven brother of today is your brother tomorrow. For this reason, you must be in a "Spirit-filled" body of believers that operate in the leading of the Holy Spirit to accurately make such discernments.

Suspicion among members, apart from genuine disclosure by the Holy Spirit, can prove to be disastrous when desperate times come. Even the Apostles experienced defection among those who once claimed to be their companions in the work of the ministry.

Jesus said we will know a person by their fruits, not their Bible knowledge; not their giving; not their heritage in ministry; nor any admirable trait.

The fruit of the Holy Spirit is produced from close fellowship with Him. Therefore, you will know them by their *fruits*. Use this as a strict criteria. Look for the characterisms of the Five Wise Virgins that are proven over time, not within a moment.

13. A list of items for your refuge needs to be formulated based on your location and the resources available in the general area where you will go. But remember, it is impractical to gather everything at once and transport it all at the same time. The list of practical items is somewhat large and must be fashioned specifically according to your skills, needs, and climate.

The supply and demand of many items ebb and flow on the market, or may become unavailable such as ammunition. Accordingly, this is a substantial project, but it is easily accomplished with many small steps starting today. In view of that task, with proper planning you can gradually over time transport the inventory of items to your location.

14. The use of pack animals, especially horses, lamas, etc., leave a discernable trail just as wild animals do. If such means of transport are used, be sure to use different routes in and out of your location with enough time between trips for the ground to recover from the tracks.

15. As previously stated, your countdown starts the day the 7-Year Peace Pact is signed. The signing will be a world heralded event. After all, Antichrist wants everyone to know he is a hero that possesses the military and economic capability to do what he claims. Accordingly, the Peace Pact will be a much advertised celebration when Antichrist's military ends the war with Israel.

16. When calculating the 1,260-Day Period, it is best to calculate by the consecutive number of days starting from the signing of the 7-Year Peace Pact. For easy computation, assume for a brief moment that the Peace Pact is signed on March 16. 1,260 days later falls on August 25. In most places, August is still a warm part of the year depending on various geographic factors specific to your location.

But if you slide the date when the Peace Pact is signed to sixty days later, then the 1,260th day is nearly at the end of November, well into the cold winter season. Therefore, you must plan to be on location much earlier than November in order to make adequate preparations for the changing seasons!

Again, with regard to the changing times and seasons, calculate by counting the consecutive number of days to determine when you need to be on location.

By considering such factors as time and season, the journey to your refuge, for example, might start on the 1,150th day from the signing of the Peace Pact in order to be on location before challenging weather arrives. Regardless, you'll want to be on location, settled in, and prepared for the seasonal changes.

But How Can You Know For Sure

The answer to that question is important. After all, the last thing you want to do is mistakenly forsake all things only to find out it was a huge oversight. Therefore, consider the collective evidence of the following events in their proper order. By doing this, it is extremely improbable that you will make any mistake by over-reacting on a singular misapplied event:

1. Look for a definitive 3-Nation Coalition headed up by a single man.

2. Watch for a world war event that involves Israel when she is overwhelmed by forces.

3. Look for the nation that offers Israel a well-publicized 7-Year Peace Pact—the same nation that heads up the Nation Coalition.

After You Are On Location—More Confirmations

1. Listen on your radios for the event that describes Antichrist breaking covenant with Israel.

2. Listen on your radio that heralds Antichrist's claim of being God.

3. Listen on your radio about the world being in awe of the False Prophet's power.

4. Listen on your radios for the mandate to receive the Mark of the Beast and the order to make an image of Antichrist and worship it.

5. Listen on your radios for news broadcasts referring to the two prophets speaking from the city of Jerusalem.

6. Listen on your radios of the current events of Antichrist's global campaign to kill all the non-conformists.

In this Critical Truth #8, you are faced with the urgency of time in preparation. Your escape to the wilderness requires serious considerations in finding a location matched with your skills, abilities, and specific needs. Use this time to develop such skills specific to the area you've selected.

To accurize your preparation, you must visit the area in order to confirm the particulars. Therefore, you must scout the land to learn the climate, water sources, food types, shelter options, and the coverage for staying hidden. Ideally, if you find a geothermic source, it would be greatly beneficial.

Selecting those who will be with you requires that you know them by the Holy Spirit, and that you trust them. It takes time to discover their character and depth in Christ. It could be a fatal mistake to share your location and intentions with those who potentially might become your enemy in the Endtimes. The time of preparation for all things is NOW.

CHAPTER 9
CRITICAL TRUTH #9

What Happens After the Rapture?

In this final Critical Truth, you will discover what Scripture describes as the unquenchable wrath of God. The chaos that follows the Rapture will be a time unlike anything that has ever existed. It will be so severe that the Bible says people will have cardiac failure from fear alone.

> Men's hearts failing them for fear, and for looking after [anticipating with all certainty] those things which are coming on the earth: for the powers of heaven shall be shaken. 27 And then shall they see the Son of man coming in a cloud with power and great glory. 28 And when these things begin to come to pass, then look up, and lift up your heads; for your redemption draweth nigh.
> Luke 21-26-28 (Square brackets inserted by the author for clarity of context.)

Pertaining to those left behind after the Rapture, some will still have the opportunity to give their lives to Jesus, but only if they have not received the Mark of the Beast. For those who have taken the Mark, there is no hope. It is an unforgivable sin ending in eternal damnation.

In all truth, no one will have an excuse for rejecting the Lord's offer of salvation. Regarding that truth, consider the evidence of God's efforts to save mankind.

First, He sent Jesus Christ—the most publicized name in all humanity. Jesus said the end would not come until the Gospel was preached to all nations. Therefore, by the time He redeems His people at the Rapture, every nation will have heard the Gospel and the saving news He offered them.

Second, well b*efore* Jesus returns at the time of the 6th Seal, especially during Seals 1 through 3, there will be a massive move of the Holy Spirit with indisputable extraordinary signs and wonders that testify of God's undeniable mercy and grace. The world will see mass healings, resurrections from the dead, limbs growing out; body parts restored; and the profuse evidence and operation of the nine gifts of His Holy Spirit (I Corinthians 12). Even some of the most hardened people will humble themselves before Jesus and give their lives to Him.

Third, before the Mark of the Beast is imposed upon the global masses, God sends three angels around the world that proclaim one last warning not to take the Mark or to worship the image of Antichrist. The last angel's message is most specific in the warning:

Then another angel, a third one, followed them, saying with a loud voice, "If anyone worships the Beast and his image, and receives a mark on his forehead or on his hand, 10 he also will drink of the wine of the wrath of God, which is mixed in full strength in the cup of His anger; and he will be tormented with fire and brimstone in the presence of the holy angels and in the presence of the Lamb.11 And the smoke of their torment goes up forever and ever; they have no rest day and night, those who worship the Beast and his image, and whoever receives the mark of his name." Revelation 14:9-11

Despite this supernatural warning, some will ignore it and receive the Mark of the Beast thus sealing themselves unto eternal damnation. Their choice is irreversible and it cannot be forgiven. Their reality is this: they only have 1,335 days of life mixed with the judgments of God in a chaotic desperate world before they are cast in to hell.

After The Rapture Takes Place

The Rapture occurs at the time of the 6th Seal. But recall that the two Endtime prophets, Enoch and Elijah, come down from Heaven between the 3rd and 4th Seal before the Mark of the Beast is required. They will be voices of woe and warning against taking the Mark.

179

They are invincible and for 1,260 days they prophesy and perform miraculous unstoppable works until the time of the 6th Trumpet Judgment. At that time, they will be allowed by God to be martyred. They will lay in the streets of Jerusalem for three and one-half days as the world celebrates their death. Then, on the 4th day, they are Raptured into Heaven.

In regard of all that, when Jesus comes at the time of the 6th Seal, the two prophets will already have been telling the world of His soon coming and the signs that proceed His arrival. Accordingly, when the world sees the sky peel back like a scroll and Jesus coming on the clouds, they know "The Day of the Lord" has come with an indescribable fury. Anticipating God's wrath, they scream in panic:

> I looked when He broke the sixth seal, and there was a great earthquake; and the sun became black as sackcloth {made} of hair, and the whole moon became like blood; 13 and the stars of the sky fell to the earth, as a fig tree casts its unripe figs when shaken by a great wind. 14 The sky was split apart like a scroll when it is rolled up, and every mountain and island were moved out of their places **[but not eliminated until the 7th Bowl Judgment]**. 15 Then the kings of the earth and the great men and the commanders and the rich and the strong and every slave and free man hid themselves in the

caves and among the rocks of the mountains; 16 and they said to the mountains and
to the rocks, "Fall on us and hide us from the
presence of Him who sits on the throne, and
from the wrath of the Lamb; 17 for the great
day of their wrath has come, and who is able
to stand?" Revelation 6:12-17 (Square brackets inserted
by the author for clarity of context.)

All On The Same Day

The 6th Seal is the time Jesus Raptures the Saints; the 7th Seal, lasts only about 30 minutes and is immediately followed by the 1st Trumpet Judgment—all of which happen on the same day.

Again, recall the six signs the precede Jesus coming, all of which happen on the same day:

1. A great earthquake, where every island and mountain is moved out of its place.
2. The Sun will turn black as sackcloth.
3. The moon will turn blood red.
4. The stars will fall from the skies (likely a meteorite shower).
5. The sky will peel back like a scroll and they will see Jesus coming on the clouds.
6. A trumpet assigned strictly to the Rapture event will blast and the Saints will be taken.

It is quite possible that the signs of the 6th Seal take a good portion of a single day based upon the appearances of the sun, moon, and stars. However, after the Saints are taken, the next two events: the 7th Seal and 1st Trumpet Judgment, occur immediately one after the other.

The Woes

As you read about the Seals and the Trumpet and Bowl Judgments in Appendix 2, and 3 you will notice there are three "Woes".

The "Woes" are warnings, *announcements* of the amplified severe judgments yet to come. It is given to those who still have the opportunity to turn to Jesus if they have not yet taken the Mark of the Beast. But for those who have taken the Mark of the Beast, they will experience even more torment for their choice of refusing Jesus and choosing Antichrist.

Remember, that from the opening of the 1st Seal, Antichrist has duped the world with his humanistic and Satanic inspired powers. However, like any man, he is limited. Not even Satan has unlimited power. Accordingly, from the 1st Seal to the 6th Seal, it will seem to the world that Antichrist's claim of being God is exactly as the False Prophet announced.

There is a reason, however, in defiance of common sense, that Antichrist's disciples believe him. They are bonded and thus blinded to a lie because they did not love the truth.

[The lawless one is coming] that is, the one whose coming is in accord with the activity

of Satan, with all power and signs and false wonders, 10 and with all the deception of wickedness for those who perish, because they did not receive the love of the truth so as to be saved. 11 For this reason God will send upon them a deluding influence so that they will believe what is false, 12 in order that they all may be judged who did not believe the truth, but took pleasure in wickedness.
II Thessalonians 2: 9-12 (Square brackets inserted by the author for clarity of context.)

Once God's judgments begin, Antichrist's public profile is destroyed. He transforms from a prolific world conquering champion to a humiliating defensive loser.

When God's fury is released upon the wicked masses, they will look to their leader who is incapable of stopping God, and they will see that he is no match against God's powers. A hopelessness among the Antichrist disciples will increase exponentially as judgments become more and more severe.

The rest of mankind, who were not killed by these plagues **[judgments of God]**, did not repent of the works of their hands, so as not to worship demons, and the idols of gold and of silver and of brass and of stone and of wood, which can neither see nor hear nor

walk; 21 and they did not repent of their murders, nor of their sorceries, nor of their immorality, nor of their thefts. Revelation 9:20-21
(Square brackets and underline inserted by the author for clarity of context.)

The 5th Trumpet Judgment is the *First Woe*. In this judgment, indescribable creatures arise from the Abyss and cover the earth. They target only those with the Mark of the Beast and inflict relentless excruciating pain for five months, day and night, without ceasing. Antichrist's disciples will try killing themselves to escape the torment. Suicide, however, is not an option. By the edict of God, it is impossible for them to die regardless of what they try in order to end their lives.

The 6th Trumpet Judgment is the *Second Woe*. A swarm of demonic creatures numbering 200,000,000 covers the earth. In a single day, they kill ⅓ of the godless masses—a number equaling close to the number of Saints that Antichrist killed during the Tribulation. The people killed by these hideous creatures are the same people who assisted Antichrist in apprehending the Saints and killing them.

Finally, the *Third Woe* is the entire 7- Bowl Judgments. They occur in rapid sequence over the next 25 days as compared to the Trumpet Judgments, only with unimaginable fury.

Leaping Forward to the Final Judgment

Leaping forward to the 7th Bowl Judgment—the final judgment, when it is completed the earth is uninhabitable. All the fresh waters are turned into blood—not figuratively, but literally; all the oceans are turned to blood in the same way, and everything in the sea dies (Revelation 16:3); the cities and mountains are leveled and the islands are erased. The earth is desolate for the most part.

After this, God takes a 45-day period of time and restores the earth to her former pristine condition similar to the days of Adam. Scripture does not explain why Jesus takes this long, but at the end of the 45 days the earth is restored. On the following day, Jesus holds a special court known as the "Sheep and Goat Judgment". This is for all those who gave their lives to Him "after" the Rapture. This will also include Antichrist's disciples who somehow managed to survive the Lord's wrath.

Those who accepted Jesus are ushered into the 1,000-Year Rule of His kingdom where He presides over the earth from His throne in Jerusalem. And those who refused to accept Him but somehow managed to survive the judgments, are cast into hell. This also includes those with the Mark of the Beast.

Going back again to the Five Foolish Virgins that were left behind at the time of the Rapture but who refused to deny Jesus and were martyred by Antichrist, they are resurrected on the 1st day of the Millennium.

> And I {saw} the souls of those who had been beheaded because of their testimony of Jesus and because of the Word of God, and those who had not worshiped the Beast or

his image, and had not received the mark on their forehead and on their hand; and they came to life and reigned with Christ for a thousand years. Revelation 20:4b (Underline by author.)

Satan Is Bound for 1,000 Years

On the first day of Jesus' 1,000-Year Reign on earth, Satan is bound by a chain and locked away in the Abyss for the entire 1,000 years.

At the end of the Millennium, he is loosed for a short period of time. He will cover the earth looking for those who will follow him—specifically the people who are untested and unproven that were born during the 1,000-Year Rule of Jesus. This is the 5th Cycle of Evil and the final battle for all of eternity.

Scripture offers very little detail about this event. However, according to the Bible, Satan and those who choose to follow him are consumed by fire from Heaven and then cast into the Lake of Fire.

At the final judgment for all time—The White Throne Judgment of God, the dead (which includes everyone in hell), is brought before God and the books of their lives are opened. They are judged based upon their works in the days of their lives on earth. The degree of their punishment is measured accordingly and they are cast alive into the Lake of Fire.

After the end of the White Throne Judgment, the Saints are ushered into eternity with God our Father who will infinitely display His glory as we enjoy His presence and experience His love forever. This is a time where the greatness of our Father is unimaginable. It is impossible for anyone to conceive the great things He has planned for the Saints.

> "But as it is written: '"Eye has not seen, nor ear heard, nor have entered into the heart of man the things which God has prepared for those who love Him."' I Corinthians 2:9

The Nine Critical Truths

While a great deal more can be detailed of each Critical Truth, the final part belongs to you. You must give serious consideration to each truth and weave them into the fabric of your life. Pray that the Holy Spirit will give you an ever deepening understanding of them.

Your best defense is to wholly rely upon God's wisdom, strength, and guidance. In any case, you must develop a deeper fellowship with Him that is more than academic knowledge concerning these nine Critical Truths. To do that, you must dedicate routine times in the study of His Word along with regular times of prayer, and personal worship. It is vitally important that you maintain a consistent close fellowship with like-minded Saints.

It is my sincere hope that you give sober consideration to these truths found in the Word of God—not as the words of man's logic, or man's philosophical view of a religious perspective, but by the very power of God's Word that gives ample warning and understanding to our generation.

Some will find these to be controversial and even argumentative. Don't be surprised by this reaction. These are the same mentalities that existed in the days of Noah who thought he was a fool. He reached beyond his day into something never before considered that was void of any historic reference. These, however, are the days Jesus described when He said:

> Truly I say to you, this generation will not pass away until all these things take place. 35 Heaven and earth will pass away, but My Words will not pass away. 36 But of that day and hour no one knows, not even the angels of Heaven, nor the Son, but the Father alone. 37 For the coming of the Son of Man will be just like the days of Noah. 38 For as in those days before the flood they were eating and drinking, marrying and giving in marriage, until the day that Noah entered the ark, 39 and they did not understand until the flood came and took them all away; so will the coming of the Son of Man be. Matthew 24:34-39

In this Critical Truth #9, the reality of God's Kingdom is knowing His plan—plans according to Bible prophecy made available to all who seek the truth. Sadly, you will

have friends and even families who find your urgency in Jesus as something of *no serious consideration*. To them, it is a story of unbelief having no proximity of reality for their lives today.

Even worse, they might be the same ones who later accept the Mark of the Beast. What becomes of them will not be easy to accept. But remember, this burden belongs to the Lord who desires they turn to Him. We can only hope in God's grace to accept the demise of those whom we know and love that will incur God's wrath.

Doubtless, this is a lot to process. It is a time when the supernatural interfaces with the natural where we will see things never before experienced. Such were the surprises of those during Noah's days and even in the days of Jesus' earthly ministry when people proclaimed that no one had ever seen such marvelous works.

So shall it be during our days as well. The things we will see and experience have no historical precedence. Only those who are spiritually minded will grasp the concept.

May the Lord enrich you in all wisdom and understanding specific to your life, your needs, and the things you must be doing *now* in the fellowship of the Holy Spirit for you to be prepared for the things soon to come by the prophetic fulfillment of our days.

En Agape,

Don Kremer

Appendix 1

OVERVIEW
FIVE CYCLES OF EVIL

1st Cycle—Satan's Fall and Intentions
Isaiah 14:12-17 ; Luke 10:18

In this first cycle, Satan attempts to usurp God by vying for His glory and to be worshipped as God. Satan stages a rebellion in Heaven and is violently cast to the earth as a bolt of lightning. He comes to the earth as a wandering spirit without authority or purpose. This cycle runs from the moment of Satan's fall to the Garden of Eden.

2nd Cycle—Satan Steals Adam's Dominion
Genesis 2:16-17; Genesis 3

Satan was cast to the earth, and is called the god of the air (Eph 2:2).

Knowing Adam and Eve have dominion over the earth, and knowing they are created in the image of God, Satan sets his focus upon stealing their dominion. He creates a set of circumstances through the trickery of temptation to bring about Adam's fall. When Adam fails, by default, he surrenders his God-given dominion and authority to Satan who assumes Adam's authority. The state of the earth falls under a curse consistent to the nature of Satan.

After Adam's fall, God announces the coming of the Messiah (Genesis 3:15) through the seed of woman. This second cycle runs from the Garden of Eden to the time of the global flood of Noah's day.

3rd Cycle—The Flood to the Tower of Babel
Genesis 6:1-8 ; Jude 1:6-7

The lineage of the coming Messiah—Jesus Christ, according to prophecy, had to come through the "seed of woman". Satan therefore, set a plan into motion to pollute the human lineage by sending his fallen angels to mate with the daughters of men. A hybrid race of people are created known as the Nephilim—giants on the earth (Genesis 6). The earth is filled with wickedness as the hybrid race multiply.

As Satan sets out to destroy the genetic design of humanity in order to stop the Messiah, the hybrid race grows exceedingly numerous and influential. The earth is saturated in corruption except for eight righteous people—Noah and his family—pedigree humans through which the Messiah comes. Noah's sons, Shem, Ham, and Jephthah, along with their wives, will restart the populations of humanity. Accordingly, the Messiah eventually comes through Shem's lineage. This cycle runs from the time of the flood to the Tower of Babel.

4th Cycle—Mankind Evolves Independent of God
Genesis 11:1-9

Satan attempts to bring about global humanism and establishes a plethora of religious beliefs through the doctrines of demons (I Timothy 4:1). He again introduces a hybrid lineage as he did before. This time, however, God judges the angels who transformed themselves into men of common flesh and chained them in darkness so they can no longer leave their spiritual domain (Jude 1:7).

"Mystery Babylon" under Nimrod is created which begins Sun Worship (Baal religion). Man seeks independence from God and chooses to go his own spiritual way.

As mankind increases on the earth, they collectively remained in the plains of Shinar instead of scattering throughout the earth to subdue it.

God confounds their unified gathering by confusing their languages and scattering them across the globe. Thus, begins the development of nations and races of people.

This cycle runs from the Tower of Babel to the beginning of the Millennial Rule of Jesus Christ which encompasses our generation. In this cycle of evil, Antichrist comes and demands global worship. This is the cycle where Satan temporarily reaches his goal to be worshipped along with his cohort, Antichrist. This is the most treacherous cycle of all where ¼ of mankind is killed for refusing to worship them. You are presently living near the end of this cycle just before the mandate of Satanic worship begins.

5th Cycle—Satan's Final Rebellion on Earth
Revelation 20:7-12

On the first day of the Millennium of Jesus' rule on earth (1,336 days later, starting from the 4th Seal), Satan is locked away in the Abyss for 1,000 years. The earth will live in true peace and prosperity as the populations of mankind increase once more. With Satan locked away, however, those who are born during the 1,000 years are untested and unproven in their choice between good and evil. At the end of the 1,000 years, Satan is released from the Abyss. Knowing this is his last opportunity to defeat God, he furiously covers the earth gathering whomever will follow him.

This final battle has very little information given in Scripture. Nonetheless, Satan and his cohorts are destroyed by fire from God's throne and cast into the Lake of Fire.

Appendix 2
OVERVIEW OF THE TRUMPET JUDGMENTS
The 7th Seal and 1st Trumpet Judgment

Recall that at the 5th Seal, the martyred Saints of Antichrist's Tribulation cry out to God. They are described as the souls under the altar of God:

> When he opened the fifth seal, I saw under the altar the souls of those who had been slain because of the word of God and the testimony they had maintained. 10 They called out in a loud voice, "How long, Sovereign Lord, holy and true, until you judge the inhabitants of the earth and avenge our blood?" 11Then each of them was given a white robe, and they were told to wait a little longer, until the full number of their fellow servants, their brothers and sisters, were killed just as they had been. Revelation 8:9-11

At the time of the 7th Seal (which is minutes apart from the time of the 1st Trumpet Judgment), the events will almost seem as part of the Trumpet Judgment. However, this is the moment God answers the prayers of the Saints, under the altar of the 5th Seal:

Another angel came and stood at the altar, holding a golden censer; and much incense was given to him, so that he might add it to the prayers of all the saints on the golden altar which was before the throne. 4 And the smoke of the incense, with the prayers of the saints, went up before God out of the angel's hand. 5 Then the angel took the censer and filled it with the fire of the altar, and threw it to the earth; and there followed peals of thunder and sounds and flashes of lightning and an earthquake. Revelation 8:3-5

1st Trumpet Judgment—Revelation 8:7

And the first sounded, and there came hail and fire, mixed with blood, and they were thrown to the earth; and a ⅓ of the earth was burned up, and a ⅓ of the trees were burned up, and all the green grass was burned up.

2nd Trumpet Judgment—Revelation 8:8-9

The second angel sounded, and something like a great mountain burning with fire was thrown into the sea; and a third of the sea became blood, 9 and a ⅓ of the creatures which were in the sea and had life, died; and a third of the ships were destroyed.

3rd Trumpet Judgment—Revelation 8:10-11

The third angel sounded, and a great star fell from heaven, burning like a torch, and it fell on a third of the rivers and on the springs of waters. 11 The name of the star is called Wormwood; and a third of the waters became wormwood, and many men died from the waters, because they were made bitter.

4th Trumpet Judgment—Revelation 8:12

The fourth angel sounded, and a ⅓ of the sun and a ⅓ of the moon and a ⅓ of the stars were struck, so that a ⅓ of them would be darkened and the day would not shine for a ⅓ of it, and the night in the same way.

Announcement of the "Woes"—Revelation 8:13

Then I looked, and I heard an eagle flying in mid-heaven, saying with a loud voice, "Woe, woe, woe to those who dwell on the earth, because of the remaining blasts of the trumpet of the three angels who are about to sound!"

The "Woes" are warnings equally as much for those who have not taken the Mark of the Beast as for those who have not given their lives to Jesus Christ. With special emphasis, however, it is an announcement of God's continued fury against all who have received the Mark of the Beast. For them, there is no mercy, only judgment.

The First "Woe" warns of the very next Trumpet Judgment—the 5th. This judgment brings hideous creatures so monstrous that it is difficult to describe them in terms of anything we have on the earth. It lasts for 5 months and is inflicted upon only those who have received the Mark of the Beast. The pain is so excruciating that Antichrist's disciples cannot mentally or physically handle the unceasing torment. They will seek suicide as a means of escape but God has made it impossible for them to die.

The Second "Woe" is the start the 6th Trumpet Judgment. This includes the army of 200,000,000 (two hundred million) creatures that arise out of the Abyss killing ⅓ of mankind and ends after Enoch and Elijah are martyred at the time of the 6th Trumpet Judgment.[30]

By contrast and design, the first four Trumpet Judgments are levied against the environment. The final three Trumpet Judgments are levied against the bodies of Antichrist's followers.

---

[30] The 6th Trumpet Judgment is explained in a compendium of explanations starting from Revelation 10 through 15. As such, the reader should understand that the chronological order of the Book of Revelation follows from Chapter 1 through Chapter 9. After Chapter 9, compartments of explanations are given relative within the Trumpet and Bowl Judgments.

5th Trumpet Judgment—Revelation 9:1-12

Then the fifth angel sounded, and I saw a star from heaven which had fallen to the earth; and the key of the bottomless pit was given to him. 2 He opened the bottomless pit, and smoke went up out of the pit, like the smoke of a great furnace; and the sun and the air were darkened by the smoke of the pit. 3 Then out of the smoke came locusts upon the earth, and power was given them, as the scorpions of the earth have power. 4 They were told not to hurt the grass of the earth, nor any green thing, nor any tree, but only the men who do not have the seal of God on their foreheads *[meaning the 144,000 Jews in hiding are protected from this judgment]*. 5 They were told not to hurt the grass of the earth, nor any green thing, nor any tree, but only the men who do not have the seal of God on their foreheads. 6 And in those days men will seek death and will not find it; they will long to die, and death flees from them. 7 The appearance of the locusts was like horses prepared for battle; and on their heads appeared to be crowns like gold, and their faces were like the faces of men. 8 They had hair like the hair of women, and their teeth were like the teeth of lions. 9 They had breastplates like breastplates of iron; and the sound of their wings was like the sound of chariots, of many horses rushing to battle. 10 They have tails like scorpions, and stings; and in their tails is their power to hurt men for five months. 11 They have as king over them, the angel of the abyss; his name in Hebrew is Abaddon, and in the Greek he has

198

the name Apollyon. 12 The first woe is past; behold, two woes are still coming after these things. (Square brackets by the author inserted for clarity.

6ᵗʰ Trumpet Judgment—Revelation 9:13-19

Then the sixth angel sounded, and I heard a voice from the four horns of the golden altar which is before God, 14 one saying to the sixth angel who had the trumpet, "Release the four angels who are bound at the great river Euphrates." 15 And the four angels, who had been prepared for the hour and day and month and year, were released, so that they would kill a third of mankind. 16 The number of the armies of the horsemen was two hundred million; I heard the number of them. 17 And this is how I saw in the vision the horses and those who sat on them: the riders had breastplates the color of fire and of hyacinth and of brimstone; and the heads of the horses are like the heads of lions; and out of their mouths proceed fire and smoke and brimstone. 18 A third of mankind was killed by these three plagues, by the fire and the smoke and the brimstone which proceeded out of their mouths. 19 For the power of the horses is in their mouths and in their tails; for their tails are like serpents and have heads, and with them they do harm. 20 The rest of mankind, who were not killed by these plagues, did not repent of the works of their hands, so as not to worship demons, and the idols of gold and of silver and of brass and of stone and of wood, which can neither see nor hear nor walk; 21 and they did not repent of their murders nor of their sorceries nor of their immorality nor of their thefts.

7th Trumpet Judgment—Revelation 11:15-19

The 7th Trumpet is a declaration in Heaven but with almost no penalty of judgment associated with it on earth. In verse 19, it speaks of a great earthquake with lightening, thunder, and a hailstorm, but the effects are not quantified in damage upon the earth. Accordingly, the 7th Trumpet entails the completion of judgment against Israel from the time of her apostasy, specifically the completion of the 70th Week of Daniel's prophecy.

Appendix 3
OVERVIEW OF THE BOWL JUDGMENTS

As compared to the Trumpet Judgments, the Bowl Judgments are intense and occur in rapid sequence. In fact, they are administered over the span of 25 days as compared to the 5th Trumpet Judgment that lasts for five months.

The Third "Woe" is all seven Bowl Judgment—with the 7th Bowl Judgment being the most destructive of all. The 7th Bowl Judgment ends with the earth's environment being completely destroyed where the seas and waters are turned to blood; all life dies in the seas; the islands are erased through tsunamis; the mountains are leveled by earthquakes; the cities are shaken to the ground; and masses of people are killed by 100 pound hail stones falling to the earth at over 120 MPH.

1st Bowl Judgment—Revelation 16:2

So the first angel went and poured out his bowl on the earth; and it became a loathsome and malignant sore on the people who had the mark of the beast and who worshiped his image.

2nd Bowl Judgment—Revelation 16:3

The second angel poured out his bowl into the sea, and it became blood like that of a dead man; and every living thing in the sea died.

3rd Bowl Judgment—Revelation 16:4-6

Then the third angel poured out his bowl into the rivers and the springs of waters; and they became blood. 5 And I heard the angel of the waters saying, "Righteous are You, who are and who were, O Holy One, because You judged these things; 6 for they poured out the blood of saints and prophets, and You have given them blood to drink. They deserve it."

4th Bowl Judgment—Revelation 16:8-9

The fourth angel poured out his bowl upon the sun, and it was given to it to scorch men with fire. 9 Men were scorched with fierce heat; and they blasphemed the name of God who has the power over these plagues, and they did not repent so as to give Him glory.

5th Bowl Judgment—Revelation 16:10-11

Then the fifth angel poured out his bowl on the throne of the beast, and his kingdom became darkened; and they gnawed their tongues because of pain, 11 and they blasphemed the God of heaven because of their pains and their sores; and they did not repent of their deeds.

6ᵗʰ Bowl Judgment—Revelation 16:12-16

The sixth angel poured out his bowl on the great river, the Euphrates; and its water was dried up, so that the way would be prepared for the kings from the east. 13 and I saw coming out of the mouth of the dragon [Satan] and out of the mouth of the beast and out of the mouth of the false prophet, three unclean spirits like frogs; 14 for they are spirits of demons, performing signs, which go out to the kings of the whole world, to gather them together for the war of the great day of God, the Almighty. 15 ("Behold, I am coming like a thief. Blessed is the one who stays awake and keeps his clothes, so that he will not walk about naked and men will not see his shame.") 16 And they gathered them together to the place which in Hebrew is called Har-Magedon.

7ᵗʰ Bowl Judgment—Revelation 16:17-21

Then the seventh angel poured out his bowl upon the air, and a loud voice came out of the temple from the throne, saying, "It is done." 18 And there were flashes of lightning and sounds and peals of thunder; and there was a great earthquake, such as there had not been since man came to be upon the earth, so great an earthquake was it, and so mighty. 19 The great city was split into three parts, and the cities of the nations fell. Babylon the great was remembered before God, to give her the cup of the wine of His fierce wrath. 20 And every island fled away, and the mountains were not found. 21

And huge hailstones, about one hundred pounds each, came down from heaven upon men; and men blasphemed God because of the plague of the hail, because its plague was extremely severe.

Isaiah 24:20-22 Describes This Particular Earthquake:

The earth reels to and fro like a drunkard and it totters like a shack, for its transgression is heavy upon it, and it will fall, never to rise again. 21 So it will happen on that day, that the LORD will punish the *rebellious* angels of heaven on high, and the kings of the earth on earth. 22 They will be gathered together like prisoners in the dungeon, and will be confined in prison; and after many days they will be punished.

Made in the USA
Monee, IL
24 January 2023

26179160R00115